¡YA CAIGO!

PUZZLES, LOGIC GAMES AND BRAIN-TEASERS

a reading resource

Brian Young

Teacher's Book

Hodder & Stoughton

A MEMBER OF THE HODDER HEADLINE GROUP

British Library Cataloguing in Publication Data

A catalogue for this book is available from the British Library.

ISBN 0 340 57270 1

First published 1994

Impression number	10 9 8 7 6 5 4 3 2 1
Year	1998 1997 1996 1995 1994

Typeset by Transet of Coventry.
Printed in Great Britain for Hodder & Stoughton Educational, a division of Hodder Headline Plc, 338 Euston Road, London NW1 3BH by St Edmundsbury Press Ltd, Bury St Edmunds, Suffolk.

Contents

Introduction

¡Ya caigo! is a collection of assorted reading materials in Spanish, which are usable on their own or with any main Spanish course. They can be used for reinforcement of language taught in the main course, for differentiating materials for pupils of differing abilities, for additional homework, or for pupils who complete a set task before others.

The materials also offer scope for writing and, in cases where pupils can work on an activity in pairs, for listening and speaking. Units which include a writing, listening or speaking activity are flagged both in the Pupil's Book and in this Teacher's Book with the following symbols:

includes a writing activity

includes a listening activity

includes a speaking activity

Extension activities are indicated to the pupil, and further possibilities are suggested here in the Teacher's Book.

The emphasis thoughout is on reading for enjoyment and on variety. The wide variety of problem-solving activities includes solving clues, finding illogicalities, establishing connections, solving true/false puzzles and logic puzzles, and sequencing. Several types of activity involve matching: matching a text to visual material, matching two texts or finding common information in several texts, matching reported to direct speech, and matching a simplified or rewritten text to the original. In the early stages pupils are asked to use visual material and a text to solve a problem. Cloze tests, split conversations, 'jigsaw' reading and sequencing involve restoring a text which has been manipulated. In the later stages, pupils link definitions to Spanish words using deduction. They also rephrase sections of longer, more difficult passages or identify themes and opinions.

Where appropriate, authentic materials and tasks are used but this is not an inflexible principle; the aim is to provide ready-made, enjoyable materials for pre- or post-communicative language practice. All the areas of experience required by the National Curriculum are covered in **¡Ya caigo!**. Each topic is presented several times, either in the activities or in the jokes, at different levels of difficulty. (See the *National Curriculum Reference* grid on pages vi-viii.)

The activities in **¡Ya caigo!** cover all the appropriate levels and statements of attainment of the National Curriculum for reading (see the *National Curriculum Reference* grid). There is a gradual progression through the levels, although not in strict order, in the interest of variety. Language is simple at the outset and becomes progressively more demanding, and the skills of scanning and gist comprehension are also gradually introduced. In the first half of the book the instructions for the activities are in English. In the second half, Spanish instructions are introduced where they are easily comprehensible. Towards the end of the book all instructions are in Spanish.

The crossword puzzles start with relatively simple 'trellises' and progress to the standard crossword format. All the crossword puzzles are particularly valuable for vocabulary revision after a topic has been covered. Many pupils will need no help, but, depending on pupils' ability, there is an increasing amount of support which the teacher can give:
(i) Ensure all pupils undstand the clues. You could get them to tell you any words in the clues they don't understand. Help them to find the meanings by deduction or by reference to work previously done, to the glossary at the end of the unit or to a dictionary;
(ii) Discuss with pupils the meaning of *some* of the clues;
(iii) Discuss possible solutions to some of the clues;
(iv) Give a list of words related to the topic, some of which are required for the solution;
(v) Give the words needed for the solution, but in random order.

Research shows that reading is more effective when readers use strategies for acquiring the meanings of unknown, imperfectly learned or forgotten items. These communication strategies are specifically called for in the National Curriculum: 'In learning and using the target language, pupils should have regular opportunities to . . . use knowledge about language (linguistic patterns, structures, grammatical features and relationships) to infer meaning and develop their own use of language.' (*General Requirements for Programmes of Study: Opportunities, Competences and Strategies*) They are also required by several GCSE examination boards. Communication strategies are fostered at all levels of **¡Ya caigo!**. Unknown but derivable items are pointed out and strategies are suggested for deducing their meaning. Only 'unguessable' words which have not previously occurred in the book are included in the glossaries at the end of each unit.

The glossaries also provide a progressive training in dictionary skills: in units 1 to 23 all words are listed precisely as they occur in the text; from unit 24 to unit 43 verbs are given as infinitives and the gender of nouns is indicated by (*m*) and (*f*); in the remainder of the book abbreviations and other devices used in dictionaries are used: for example, (*nm*), (*vt*), etc, appear after the Spanish word, and an indication of the contexts in which the word may be used appears with the English translation so that pupils have to choose the most likely meaning from several. (See the *Notes on use of glossaries . . .*, pages 7 and 13.)

The photocopiable Copymasters at the end of this Teacher's Book enable pupils to draw or write on their own copies of maps, diagrams and grids. They are indicated by the symbol 12.

¡Ya caigo! National Curriculum Reference

Page in Pupil's Book	Unit Content	Levels and statements of attainment				Areas of experience						
		AT1 Listening	AT2 Speaking	AT3 Reading	AT4 Writing	A	B	C	D	E	F	G
2	**1 La ciudad antigua** Wayfinding	1a	2b	2a, b		✓		✓				
3	**2 ¿Abierto o cerrado?** Opening/closing times			2a, b		✓						
5	**3 La hora mundial** Time, 24-hour clock		2b*	2a	3a						✓	
6	**4 Unas postales** Information about towns			3a	2b 4b*	✓		✓			✓	
8	**5 Los números de teléfono** Telephone; numbers to 100	1a*	1b*	1a						✓		
8	**6 El bar-restaurante** Ordering food and drink	3a*	2a, b*	2a, b		✓						
10	**7 El horario de autobuses** 24-hour clock; places in town			2a, b		✓					✓	
12	**8 Los platos combinados** Eating in a cafe; numbers 100 to 1000	3a*	4a 2a, b*	2a 3a		✓	✓					
13	**9 La tienda de recuerdos** Shopping for souvenirs	3a	2b	3a, b	4b	✓			✓			
14	**10 De compras** Buying clothes; sizes, colours			3a		✓			✓			
15	**11 Correos** Post office: basic vocabulary			1a	1a			•		✓		
16	**12 Las fichas** Personal details, colours, dates			4a	4b	✓	✓					
18	**13 ¿Cuántos años tienes?** Age			3a	2b	✓	✓					
19	**14 ¡Es un disparate!** (*Presentaciones*) Personal details			3a	4b	✓	✓					
20	**15 El par de zapatos** Sizes; ordinal numbers			3a		✓						
20	**16 Familias y ciudades** Personal details; towns, houses	3a*	3a*	3a	4a		✓	✓				
21	**17 Busco un(a) compañero/a** Sports; likes/dislikes			4a		✓	✓					
23	**18 Comida loca** Food, drink, quantities, containers	1a 4a*	2a 4a*	2a, b	2a	✓						
23	**19 ¡Es un disparate!** (*Comida favorita*) Food, drink; likes/dislikes			4a, b		✓	✓					
25	**20 ¡Eres el intérprete!** (*Carta de una amiga española*) Personal details. Illness	2b	2b	4a	5a*		✓			✓		
27	**21 El hotelero tiene problemas** Booking accommodation	3a*	3a*	3a, b		✓		✓	✓			
29	**22 Mis recuerdos** Souvenirs, gifts			3a	2a	✓					✓	
30	**23 ¿Qué le parece el hotel?** Accommodation; likes/dislikes			4a	4a			✓	✓		✓	
31	**24 El juego de las iniciales: ocio** Leisure activities	1a*	1a*	3a	2a	✓						✓

*In Teacher's Book

Page in Pupil's Book	Unit Content	Levels and statements of attainment				Areas of experience						
		AT1 Listening	AT2 Speaking	AT3 Reading	AT4 Writing	A	B	C	D	E	F	G
32	**25 Los colegios de otros países** School, daily routine, time	3a 4a	2b 4b	5a, b	5a, b				✓		✓	
34	**26 Los vecinos** Family relationships, pets			3a			✓	✓				
36	**27 ¡Qué región!** Tourist information, regions			4a	5a, b			✓	✓		✓	
38	**28 Enrejado: la farmacia** Ailments			3a	2b		✓					
40	**29 ¡Es un disparate!** (*Postales*) Weather, holidays			4a	4b			✓				
42	**30 Conversación por teléfono** Planning activities	3a*	3a*	3a	3a 5b*					✓		
43	**31 Viajes** Passport, Customs, petrol station			3a	2b						✓	
44	**32 El piso** Rooms, furniture	4a*	5b*	3a				✓				
46	**33 Los horarios** School subjects; time	4a*	4a*	3a	4a*				✓			
48	**34 Crucigrama: la comida** Food and drink			3a	2b	✓						
50	**35 En el mercado** Buying food, drink; quantities			2a	2a	✓						
51	**36 ¡Eres el intérprete!** (*Carta de la Oficina de Turismo*) Campsite, youth hostel			5a 6a	7b			✓	✓		✓	
52	**37 Perdido y encontrado** Lost property, colours			4a		✓						
54	**38 La colección de monedas** Money, nationalities			4a							✓	
56	**39 ¡Es un disparate!** (*El turista inglés de compras*) Shopping in small shops			5a	5b	✓			✓		✓	
57	**40 En el Corte Inglés** Department store, souvenirs. Preterite			4a	2b	✓			✓			
59	**41 A la mesa** Eating/drinking in cafeteria			3a		✓						
60	**42 Una semana en Sevilla** Describing past holidays. Preterite	4a*	4a*	2a	7b	✓					✓	
61	**43 Teléfonos útiles** Telephone	3a*	2a*	4a						✓		
62	**44 ¿Qué es?** Communication difficulties; definitions	5a	6c	5a	7a	✓						✓
64	**45 ¿Por qué se llama así?** Towns; street names			3a	2a 5b*			✓			✓	
65	**46 Casa fundada en . . .** Small shops; years			4a				✓	✓			
66	**47 ¡Es un disparate!** (*Los hoteles recibieron cartas*) Hotel, communication difficulties			5a, b	8a	✓			✓	✓	✓	
68	**48 Los españoles viajan** Tourist information. Imperative		7c*	7a	8a				✓		✓	
69	**49 ¡Discúlpame!** Apologising. Object pronoun			6a			✓					

*In Teacher's Book

Page in Pupil's Book	Unit Content	Levels and statements of attainment				Areas of experience						
		AT1 Listening	AT2 Speaking	AT3 Reading	AT4 Writing	A	B	C	D	E	F	G
71	**50 ¿Quién espera a quién?** Travel by train. Preterite			4a		✓		✓				
72	**51 El árbol genealógico** Introductions; family relationships			3a			✓					
73	**52 Horóscopo** Personal life. Future tense. Imperative			2a 7a, 8c	8a, b*		✓					
75	**53 En consigna** Lost property, communication difficulties			2c 6a	3b*	✓			✓			
76	**54 Corazonadas** Personal life			9b 10a			✓					✓
78	**55 Crucigrama: el ocio** Leisure interests			5a	2b 3a*	✓						✓
81	**56 Publicidad en el metro** Travel by underground; shopping			6a	2a	✓		✓	✓			
82	**57 ¡Eres el intérprete!** (*Las sugerencias de Conchita*) Accepting/declining invitations	8a*	8b*	7a	9a, b		✓					
84	**58 La comida del antaño** Food. Past tenses			7b, 8b 10a		✓	✓				✓	
86	**59 Las profesiones** Careers	2a* 8a*	9b*	9a, b					✓			
90	**60 ¿Cuándo se dice eso?** Introductions, invitations, exclamations			4a			✓	✓				
91	**61 Las carreras** Careers, training			8a	3a				✓			

***In Teacher's Book**

Areas of experience

A Everyday activities
B Personal and social life
C The world around us
D The world of education, training and work
E The world of communications
F The international world
G The world of imagination and creativity

Notes on the units

1 La ciudad antigua
page 2

Encourage and, if necessary, help pupils to work out the meanings of *tuerza*, *luego* and *otra vez*, rather than have them look them up in the glossary straight away.

If any have difficulty getting started, explain that it helps to try the first few instructions in each set at each *Puerta*, to see which one to start from. When crossing the *Plaza*, they should go straight across.

Pupils can draw the routes on their copies of the map.

►► Solution

North to South: 6
South to North: 3

►► Extension

The vocabulary items *tuerza* and *tome* are very useful in classroom work:

- At the beginning of the lesson, pupils can be asked to obey only commands preceded by *Simón dice*:
  – *Simón dice «Levántate»*
  – *Simón dice «Tuerza a la derecha»*
  – *Simón dice «Tuerza a la izquierda»*
  – *Simón dice «Siéntate»*, etc.
- Wayfinding can be practised by having one pupil direct another to a 'mystery destination' in the classroom while giving the instructions in Spanish. The spaces between furniture can be *calles*, giving scope for *Tome la primera calle a la derecha*, etc.

2 ¿Abierto o cerrado?
page 3

►► Solution

The best solution, with approximate times, is:

1	Bank	12.05	**6**	Cinema	15.00
2	Post office	12.20	**7**	Aquapark	16.00
3	Caves	12.25	**8**	Museum	18.00
4	Gardens	13.10 (eat)	**9**	Restaurant	19.00
5	Castle	14.00	**10**	Disco	20.00

It is not possible to visit the swimming pool.

►► Extension

After tracing their route on the photocopiable map, pupils can subsequently use the map for further work on wayfinding by asking each other the way to and from various places.

3 La hora mundial
page 5

Pupils need to be quite familiar with both the 12-hour and 24-hour clocks. Check that they can cope successfully with A, B and C before proceeding to D and E.

►► Solution and Extension

For pair work, pupils can ask their partners to say the answers in Spanish:

A **1** *En Los Angeles son las tres de la mañana.*
2 *En Sydney son las nueve de la tarde.*
3 *En Delhi son las cuatro y media de la tarde.*

B **1** *En Londres son las diez de la mañana.*
2 *En Tokio son las siete de la tarde.*
3 *En Alaska es medianoche.*

C **1** *En México son las diez de la mañana.*
2 *En Delhi son las nueve y media de la tarde.*
3 *En Montevideo es la una de la tarde.*

D **1** *En Madrid son las siete de la tarde.*
2 *En Madrid son las cinco de la mañana.*
3 *En Madrid es la una de la tarde.*

E **1** *En Nueva York son las siete de la mañana.*
2 *En Nueva York son las doce y media de la tarde.*
3 *En Nueva York son las once de la tarde.*

4 Unas postales
page 6

There is some unknown vocabulary in the text but a large proportion of it is ascertainable from its similarity to English.

Not all items described in the text are necessarily shown on the cards, and some background knowledge helps but is not essential. There are sufficient clues in the text to identify the cards referred to.

►► Solution

1 Torremolinos (B) **3** Sevilla (D)
2 Alicante (C) **4** Mojácar (A)

There are also many phrases in the texts which help in constructing the messages for the Barcelona and Malgrat cards. Build these up orally first. Weaker pupils can be further helped by Copymaster 3. (Possible answers: Barcelona – *turistas y hoteles/sitios de interés; plaza de toros; tráfico.* Malgrat – *costa; pintoresco; montañas; mar; barca.*)

►► Extension

Pupils can go on to work in pairs. Each writes a message which could have been written by a Spanish visitor to a local town. He or she then reads it to his or her partner who must guess which town it is.

5 Los números de teléfono
page 8

The aim is to practise the Spanish system of quoting telephone numbers in pairs of digits. (Where the number consists of an odd number of digits, a single digit is said at the beginning.) The aim is also to familiarise pupils with the written forms of the numbers. All too often, when reading aloud, pupils stumble over numbers because they are not sufficiently familiar with the words which form the numbers. Seeing them in writing can help memorisation.

Ask more able pupils to write as many of the answers as they can in English.

►► Solution

(answers in English)

1 'Rocky' disco	**6** San Carlos Hotel
2 Tourist Office	**7** Bus station
3 Post Office	**8** Railway station
4 Bank of Bilbao	**9** 'Tirita' pharmacy
5 Andalusian restaurant	**10** Museum of Art

►► Extension

Ask each pupil to write a telephone number, in figures, on two small pieces of paper. (The same number on each piece.) Each pupil keeps one copy and gives the other to you. You shuffle all your copies and read them out, one at a time. The pupil whose number is called responds by saying *¡Dígame!*

Pupils then work in pairs, saying either real or imaginary telephone numbers for their partner to write down.

6 El bar-restaurante
page 8

The following are probably the best equivalents of some items:

descafeinado: decaffeinated coffee
refrescos: cold drinks
zumos naturales: fruit juices
bollería: pastries

Explain what *anís*, *tapas* and *platos combinados* are, if necessary. The French *apéritif* is best for *aperitivo*, and *liqueur* for *licor*.

The **¿Verdad o mentira?** exercise involves knowledge of comparatives.

►► Solutions

Kevin: set meal (475), coffee (100)
Paul: pastry (170), fruit juice (75)
Tracey: tea (90), sandwich (200)

¿Verdad o mentira?

1 *Verdad*	**3** *Verdad*	**5** *Verdad*
2 *Mentira*	**4** *Mentira*	**6** *Verdad*

►► Extension

Give pupils open-ended questions, such as *Sois cuatro y tenéis 1.500 pesetas. ¿Qué podéis comprar?*

7 El horario de autobuses
page 10

Llegada and *salida* on the timetable should help pupils to work out *llega a* and *sale de* in the statements. You could also encourage them to work out the meanings of *Ciudad Universitaria, centro comercial, Pueblo Nuevo, Hipermercado Mamut*, and *todas las paradas* (see no. 4).

►► Solutions

¿Verdad o mentira?

1 *Mentira*	**5** *Verdad*	**9** *Verdad*
2 *Mentira*	**6** *Mentira*	**10** *Verdad*
3 *Verdad*	**7** *Verdad*	
4 *Verdad*	**8** *Mentira*	

Seeing the times of the day in words in the **¿Verdad o mentira?** numbers 2, 8 and 9 helps to remind pupils of how the numbers are said and practises conversion from the 24-hour to the 12-hour clock.

The correct order of sentences is:
No. 5 llega a la estación. (10.15)
No. 5 pasa por el Pueblo Nuevo. (10.36)
No. 8 pasa por el cine. (10.42)
No. 8 llega a la estación de RENFE. (11.05)
No. 5 llega a la playa. (11.10)
No. 8 sale del centro comercial. (11.40)
No. 12 pasa por la Calle Sto. Domingo. (12.55)
No. 13 sale de la estación de autobuses. (13.40)
No. 13 pasa por la Calle Ganivet. (13.45)
No. 12 pasa por el puerto. (13.57)

▸▸ Extension

The activity leads to speaking: pupils ask their partners questions beginning *¿A qué hora llega/sale ...?* or *¿El autobús número ... pasa por / va a ...?*

8 Los platos combinados
page 12

▸▸ Solution

Sally has no. 7.
Peter has no. 5.
Andy has no. 4.
Catherine has no. 3

Before doing the speaking activity, encourage pupils to work out *¿Qué ha tomado usted?, Vamos a ver, Aquí tiene* and *la vuelta*.

9 La tienda de recuerdos
page 13

4

If necessary, encourage pupils to work out *gasta más que ..., (el) más barato/caro,* and *puedo*. You could explain that *típico* means 'typically Spanish'. Encourage pupils to write whole sentences.

The final question of the speaking activity is open-ended and gives an opportunity for abler pupils to suggest Spanish words for other souvenirs. For example: *guantes, pañuelos, muñecas, cerámica, collares, pulseras, sombreros, camisetas, porcelana, lápices, bolígrafos, castañuelas*.

With the writing of the postcard, it is advisable to go over the activity orally first. *He comprado* is in the glossary.

▸▸ Solution

Nacho compra un abanico y un cinturón.
Pili compra turrón.
Mónica compra un cinturón y un disco.
Beatriz compra postales y un bolso.
Paco compra turrón y un abanico (or *postales*).

10 De compras
page 14

5

If necessary, explain *talla más grande/pequeña*. It should be obvious that boys do not buy dresses for themselves!

To help pupils along, you could give these hints at appropriate points, in English or Spanish:
- Luisa buys the dress (she is a girl).
- Sofía buys the red shoes. (Antonio buys something blue, Miguel buys a coat, Luisa buys a dress.)

By elimination:
- Luisa buys something white.
- Antonio buys the jacket.
- Miguel buys something black.
- The jacket is size 46.

▸▸ Solution

	Article	Size	Colour
Antonio	jacket	46	blue
Miguel	coat	42	black
Luisa	dress	44	white
Sofía	shoes	40	red

11 Correos
page 15

6

▸▸ Solution

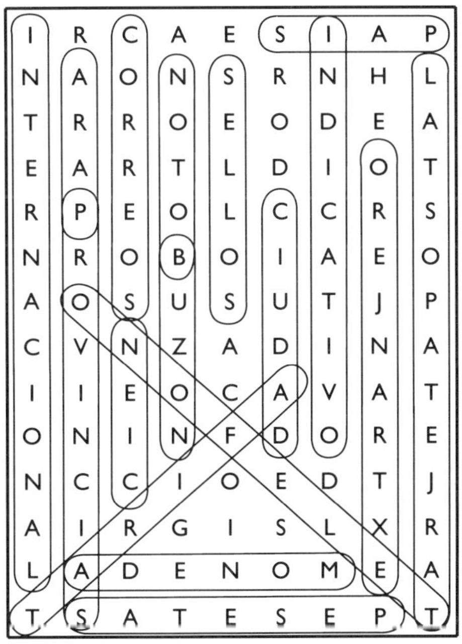

The letters left over are R, A, E, R, H, O, E, D, A, C, O, D, G, I and S. Rearranged, they form the phrase *Horas de Recogida*.

▸▸ Extension

Pupils can make their own wordsearches. They can simply add letters at random in the gaps left by the words, to form a rectangle.

12 Las fichas
page 16

7

The aims are to prepare the way for reading correspondence in Spanish, to reinforce vocabulary and structures for giving personal details, to revise colours and numbers, and to develop the skill of scanning.

Pupils fill in the details in English on the photocopiable forms.

It is a good idea to explain the Spanish system of having two surnames, for the cases where these are given. Amounts of pocket money are given in *pesetas* throughout.

▸▸ Solution

(See foot of page.)

▸▸ Extension

Pupils who finish early can proceed to work out the reasons for some of the choices given.

13 ¿Cuántos años tienes?

page 18

8

The aim is to revise vocabulary and structures for personal information (name, date of birth and where one lives or is from). Pupils write the answers on the photocopiable grid; accents are ignored.

▸▸ Solution

(See top of column opposite.)

The sentence which emerges is *Tengo diecisiete años.*

14 ¡Es un disparate!

page 19

Encourage pupils to work out the meaning of *disparate* after reading the introduction and before looking at the end.

▸▸ Solution 13 ¿Cuántos años tienes?

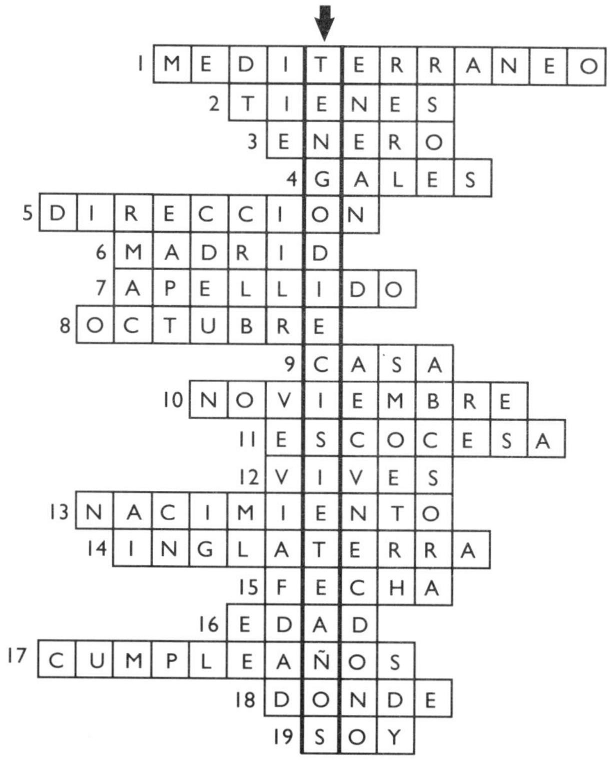

▸▸ Solution

There are several possibilities for Spanish sentences which restore the sense. If necessary discuss possibilities with the pupils and lead them towards:

1. *Mi hermano Pablo (que tiene dieciséis años) es el (hijo) mayor.*
2. *No soy hija única. / Tengo una hermana.*
3. *Tengo dieciséis años. / No es mayor que yo. / Es menor que yo.*
4. *Mis abuelos viven en la ciudad de Toledo / en la Calle de Segovia también.*

▸▸ Solution 12 Las fichas

Name	Surname(s)	Age	Nationality	Pocket money	FAVOURITE: Colour	No.	Month	Day
1 Carlos	Fuentes Pardo	14	Spanish	1.000 pts	Red	7	August	Sunday
2 Trinidad	Sandóval Martín	16	Argentinian	2.000 pts	Blue	22	February	Saturday
3 Carmen	Rosales de Soto	12	Spanish	500 pts	Green	9	April	Wednesday
4 Salvador	Treviño	*	Mexican	600 pts	Yellow	1	January	Thursday
5 Elisa	Goicoechea	15	Spanish (Basque)	1.200 pts	White	4	September	Friday

*Pupils can work back from today's date to October 1980 to determine Salvador's age.

5 *Tengo diez años. / Mi madre tiene treinta y ocho años . . . mi padre tiene treinta y nueve años. Mi madre . . . se llama Mercedes . . . mi padre se llama Ignacio.*

6 *Tengo cuatro (animales): un perro blanco, un pequeño gato negro que se llama Negrito, un pájaro en una jaula y un conejo de Indias. / . . . un pequeño perro negro que se llama Negrito / . . . un perro blanco que se llama Blanquito.*

15 El par de zapatos
page 20

Pupils should be able to work out *par* by using both contexts: shoes and Spanish telephone numbers. *Recibe* and *doble* should be easily understood. You may need to give the meaning of *da*.

►► Solution

90.84.76.54

16 Familias y ciudades
page 20

The activity encourages close reading. Many of the sentences involve comparing third person forms with first person forms. If necessary explain that *cuarto* is the general word for room by saying, for example: *El piso de Julio tiene comedor, cocina, salón y tres dormitorios: hay seis cuartos.*

►► Solution and Extension

1 Raúl
2 Karen
3 Cristina
4 Karen
5 Julio
6 Cristina
7 Karen
8 Cristina
9 Raúl
10 Julio

Discuss with the class possible questions to trigger the ten responses. According to the ability of the pupil, different possibilities often exist, eg, for number 2:

¿Vives en el este del país? or
¿En qué parte del país vives?

These questions can then be used and developed in oral pair work, with pupils taking turns to interview each other and make notes in Spanish. Finally these notes can be written up into profiles in the third person such as those in the Pupil's Book.

17 Busco un(a) compañero/a
page 21

9

To aid vocabulary acquisition, ask pupils to read the text once. Then put Copymaster 9 on the board or OHP and ask pupils to match up the jumbled meanings:

tomar parte	: to take part
algunas veces	: sometimes
nadar	: to swim
el lago	: the lake
el paseo	: the walk
la pelota	: the ball
al aire libre	: in the open air
la única cosa	: the only thing
el equipo	: the team
aficionado al tenis	: fond of tennis
ganamos	: we win

►► Solution

Francisco – Luis
Jaime – Santiago
Juana – Soledad
Felipe – Fernando
Pepe – Carlos

18 Comida loca
page 23

►► Solution

The nonsensical items are:

Una hamburguesa con gas
Un bocadillo de vino tinto
Mil kilos de patatas fritas
Churros irlandeses
Un kilómetro de salchichón
Una botella de vino azul
Gazpacho con plátanos
Medio kilo de Fanta naranja
Un helado de jamón
Una ración de queso tinto

►► Extension

Pupils, working in pairs, can produce dialogues where the 'customer' asks for several items, some of which are nonsense. When the item is sensible, the 'waiter' repeats it and says: *Muy bien*. When the item is nonsense, the waiter says: *¡Pero no hay tal cosa! ¿Quiere algo distinto?*

19 ¡Es un disparate!
page 23

If necessary tell pupils that *almuerzo* is an alternative to *comida (principal)* for 'lunch'.

►► Solution

Passage 2 has no nonsense. The nonsense in the other passages is as follows:

1 *bacalao*
chuletas
españoles
3 *jamón*
desayuno
4 *plátanos*
pescado
5 *litro*
cuarenta
no me gustan mucho las manzanas
Asturias

▸▸ Extension

To revise and expand likes and dislikes, ask pupils to pick out expressions such as:

me gusta(n) mucho
nos gusta
prefiero
preferentemente
son fenomenales
son deliciosos
mi fruta favorita
los precios son muy altos
no me gustan mucho

20 ¡Eres el intérprete!
page 25

The aim is to revise personal description and illness, and to develop the skill of gist reading.

Weaker pupils can simply identify the people in the photographs orally. All pupils should be encouraged to ignore words which they cannot work out, but *casada* should be ascertainable from the context and *tiene diez meses* is a re-combination of elements already known.

You can ask additional questions such as: 'How old is Maribel?' and 'What does *Dos Hermanas* mean?' (The town exists.)

▸▸ Solution

The most important points in the letter are:

Maribel's brother Esteban is 17, three years older than she is. He is tall, with short, dark hair and brown eyes. Her sister Pilar is 22, and married to an engineer. They have a daughter of 10 months. Maribel's younger brother Carlos is 13. He is intelligent and likes sport.

Her mother is a shop assistant. She now has long hair but in the photo it is short. Her father works in a chemist's.

Her grandparents live with them. Her grandmother is 66, and very kind. Her grandfather is 64, but looks younger because he hasn't got white hair. He is not well; his legs and feet hurt. Her father brings him medicine from the chemist's but the grandfather will probably have to go to hospital.

She asks the English friend to send photos of his/her family, and hopes that they are all well.

1 father
2 sister, Pilar
3 grandmother
4 brother
5 mother
6 brother, Esteban

▸▸ Extension

Finally, pupils could write descriptions in Spanish of members of their own families, or of famous persons, which their partners can summarise in English.

21 El hotelero tiene problemas
page 27

Encourage pupils to work out *queremos, necesito, necesitamos, escalera* and the abbreviations for *señor, señores* and *señorita*.

Pupils should begin by placing those guests whose requirements can be met exactly.

▸▸ Solution

(See foot of page 7 for the best arrangement.)

▸▸ Extension

The hotel plan can be used for 'Bingo', with each pupil choosing three rooms and the teacher or a pupil describing the rooms in random order. It can also be used for 'Noughts and Crosses'. Pupils work in pairs and score by correctly describing the room in which they wish to put their nought or cross.

22 Mis recuerdos
page 29

Accessible vocabulary is: *licor, colección, a todo color, emperador, cheques*.

▸▸ Solution

1 *una botella de coñac*
2 *una muñeca española*
3 *un mapa de Torremolinos*
4 *un paquete de postales*
5 *un bolso de piel*
6 *un folleto sobre Torremolinos*
7 *un billete de cine*
8 *un abanico*
9 *unas fotografías*
10 *una cartera de piel*

23 ¿Qué le parece el hotel?

page 30

If necessary, go through the letter to ensure that pupils understand the main points in it. *Recomendó* is in the preterite, but the connection with *recomendación* in question 1 should lead to the meaning.

Give help if necessary with the open-ended writing (questions 11 and 12), eg, giving *cuestan mucho* or *precios altos*. More able pupils can be encouraged to write more complex sentences, eg, *Me gusta especialmente porque soy muy deportista.*

Encourage the more able to note the various formulas for asking for opinions:

¿Qué opina Vd. de . . .?
¿Qué es su opinión de . . .?
¿Qué opinión tiene de . . .?
¿Qué piensa Vd. de . . .?
¿Qué le parece . . .?

►► Solution

1 Recomendación de otra persona.
2 Su precio. Sus instalaciones.
3 Malo.
4 Muy buenas.
5 Buena.
6 Malo.
7 Buena.
8 Turismo.
9 Con amigos.
10 Sí. / Hasta cierto punto.
11 Se pueden practicar muchos deportes.
12 La playa está muy lejos.

Note on use of glossaries: units 24 to 43

In units 24 to 43 the glossaries take pupils a stage further towards the use of dictionaries. The following features are used:

- Articles before nouns are replaced by (*m*) and (*f*) after the nouns.
- Only the masculine forms of adjectives are given.
- Verbs are given in the infinitive.

You could help pupils to become accustomed to these features by asking them:

1 to look at nouns in the glossaries in units 24 to 43 and to suggest what (*m*) and (*f*) stand for;
2 to tell you the words for 'a' and 'the' which would be used in front of these nouns;
3 to find some adjectives and think of feminine or plural nouns which could go with them so that the adjectives change their ending;
4 to find some verbs and create sentences changing the infinitive to a part of a tense which they know (eg, in unit 31, *olvidarse*, to forget: . . . *se olvida* . . ., . . . 'he forgets' . . .). They could then find the same verb in the body of the text and see which part of the verb was used there – in this case, *no te olvides*, 'don't forget'.

24 El juego de las iniciales: ocio

page 31

The activity can be done individually, with pupils crossing through the letters they solve and writing down what the letters stand for. For pair work, it can be a 'Blockbusters' game where

►► Solution 21 El hotelero tiene problemas

	Room no.	As requested?	Item missing?	Can't stay?
Domingo + Colón	3	✓		
Olmedo + Gracián + Quevedo	2	✓		
Gredos + Pepe	6		✓ (No balcony)	
Puente				✓
Ríos	1	✓		
Simón + Linares + Cobos	9	✓		
Callao				✓
Santos	7	✓		
Muñoz	5		✓ (No double bed)	
Rosa	4		✓ (No TV)	
González + María	8	✓		

partners take turns to state which square they are attempting. The winner is the first to go across the large square either horizontally or vertically.

Ensure that pupils understand that the clues are in a jumbled order.

►► Solution

1 TL: tiempo libre
2 EDF: equipo de fútbol
3 SDF: sala de fiestas
4 DA: deportes acuáticos
5 DUP: dar un paseo
6 CDD: centro de deportes
7 VUV: ver un vídeo
8 PZ: parque zoológico
9 CPJ: club para jóvenes

25 Los colegios de otros países

page 32

The aim is to encourage 'scanning': pupils should be encouraged to seek only the specific information required in the first instance and to ignore words which they do not understand. The use of a simple form of 'jigsaw reading' leads to speaking and listening activities. Adapting the questions to the pupils' own circumstances gives valuable practice for oral tests.

►► Solution

Collège Aristide Briand

1 Las ocho de la mañana
2 10 minutos
3 No
4 En casa; no hay cantina
5 Sí
6 A las 17.10
7 Dos
8 No
9 Sí, por la mañana
10 65
11 14
12 14

Realschule Konrad Adenauer

1 Las ocho menos cuarto
2 20 minutos
3 Sí (5 minutos)
4 En casa; no tienen que volver
5 No; hay deberes
6 No hay clases por la tarde
7 Una o dos
8 Sí
9 Sí, por la mañana
10 46
11 15
12 12

26 Los vecinos

page 34

12

New vocabulary introduced in this activity is *viuda, pares* and *impares*.

You could help pupils who are stuck by giving these clues, in Spanish or English:

- The Lorcas must live at No. 4 because they live in an even-numbered house and 2, 6 and 8 are occupied by other families.
- The Sotomayors must live at No. 6. They also live in an even-numbered house and 6 is the only one without a named family, once the Lorcas are located.
- By elimination, the Ibarras must live at No. 3.

►► Solution

House no.	Family name	Number of children	Pets
1	Blanco	2	none
2	Robles	5	2 dogs
3	Ibarra	4	canary
4	Lorca	7	4 rabbits
5	Carrero	6	dog
6	Sotomayor	none	fish
7	Tejero	3	guinea-pigs
8	Negrín	1	cat

27 ¿Qué región?

page 36

The activity deals with National Curriculum Area of Experience F: The International World, and gives useful background information about Spain. It helps pupils to become familiar with the location of the autonomous regions of Spain.

Encourage pupils to concentrate on words which they know and to start by locating the regions which they find easiest. By reference to the map and by a process of elimination they should be able to locate most or all of them.

►► Solution

1 Castilla Y León
2 Canarias
3 Cantabria
4 Cataluña
5 Asturias
6 Andalucía
7 Valencia
8 Madrid
9 Galicia
10 País Vasco
11 Murcia
12 Aragón
13 Castilla - La Mancha
14 Extremadura
15 La Rioja
16 Baleares
17 Navarra

▸▸ Extension

Ask pupils to suggest sentences in Spanish about the region in which their school or college is situated. This can be built into a composite version which would be of interest to a Spanish visitor to the region.

28 Enrejado: la farmacia

page 38

13

If necessary give the meanings of *salud, causar, cubre, resfriado, farmacéutico, aliviar, necesitas.*

Encourage pupils to seek the Spanish for 'first aid', looking under 'first' in the dictionary.

Some answers are contained in other clues, eg,
9 down in 21 across
23 across in 23 down
22 down in 24 across
18 down in 2 down

▸▸ Solution

29 ¡Es un disparate!

page 40

If necessary ask pupils to suggest corrected versions of the illogical sentences orally before they attempt to write them.

▸▸ Solutions and suggestions

No. 1 is the easiest to adapt: *esquiar* is nonsense and could change to *tomar el sol; visitar las fábricas* is very unlikely and could become *ir a las discotecas,* for example.

In no. 2, *diez* is too low and could become *treinta* and *Asturias* should of course be *Andalucía*. In the last sentence, *tengo* could be replaced by *no necesito.*

In no. 3, *la playa* is nonsense and could become *la piscina. Con mis amigos* and *en el mar* (nonsense) can be omitted, and *nevando* could be *lloviendo.*

No. 4 shows the difference between *nieve* and *niebla. Tercera semana en Londres* is illogical here and could become *próxima visita a Londres.*

In no. 5 pupils could change *la capital* (incorrect) to *una gran ciudad. Otoño* must be changed to *primavera.*

30 Conversación por teléfono

page 42

The material can be used for whole class work, pair work or individual speaking or writing activities.

You could read the part of Mercedes aloud and ask pupils to choose possible responses. Those who do not speak can be asked to judge which responses they prefer, so that a full conversation is built up.

Pupils can work in pairs, simply reading the parts. Pairs of more able pupils look at Mercedes' part only, with one partner reading Mercedes' script and the other supplying responses for Sarita which make sense. They then look at Sarita's script only and the partner who read Mercedes' script now either says it from memory or makes variations on it.

▸▸ Extension

Pupils could write and perform an extension of the conversation from . . . *junto al puesto de refrescos*. A continuation could start *¿Y después?*. Or they could write a similar split conversation for other pairs of pupils to use.

31 Viajes

page 43

14

Those pupils who have done only the regular forms of the preterite can be asked to work out the reasons for the spelling of *saqué* and *pagué.*

The activity continues the build-up to a full-scale crossword in Spanish in unit 55.

▸▸ Solution

(See next page.)

C	A	M	A	R	A
O					D
S		**1**			U
T					A
A					N
S	E	M	A	N	A

T	A	B	A	C	O
A					L
R		**2**			V
D					I
E					D
S	A	L	I	D	A

P	E	S	E	T	A
A					B
I		**3**			R
S					I
E					G
S	A	L	U	D	O

T	A	R	I	F	A
I					B
E		**4**			R
N					A
E					Z
N	U	M	E	R	O

G	R	A	N	D	E
U					S
S		**5**			P
T					A
A					Ñ
N	I	E	B	L	A

V	E	I	N	T	E
U					L
E		**6**			A
L					I
V					R
A	C	E	I	T	E

32 El piso

page 44

Encourage pupils to work out *fregadero, cada, otro* and *además de* before looking to see whether any of them are listed in the glossary.

▸▸ Solution

Description no. 4 corresponds to the plan.

▸▸ Extension

Working in pairs, one partner draws a plan of a more complex flat, with furniture, and reads a description of it in Spanish to his or her partner, who draws it. They compare drawings at the end.

33 Los horarios

page 46

▸▸ Solution

1 Rafael
2 Yolanda
3 Yolanda
4 Paloma
5 Paloma
6 Yolanda
7 Rafael
8 Rafael
9 Yolanda
10 Paloma
11 Paloma
12 Yolanda
13 Rafael
14 Paloma
15 Paloma
16 Paloma

Yolanda does most subjects and goes to a church school (she has most RE lessons).

▸▸ Extension

As the basis of a speaking activity, ask pupils as a class or individually:

¿Qué horario os/te parece mejor? ¿Por qué?
¿Qué horario se parece más al vuestro/tuyo?
¿Qué diferencias hay entre estos horarios y el de un colegio inglés?

As a writing activity, each pupil writes in Spanish a number of sentences about his or her school or college. They can include the subjects they study. You then ask pupils to read out their sentences, building up a composite version on the board or OHP.

34 Crucigrama: la comida

page 48

15

▸▸ Solution

Horizontales

1 Ensalada
5 Vino
7 Si
8 Tarta
9 Calamares
13 Melocotón
15 El aceite
16 Río
19 Bebidas
20 Él
21 Su
22 Flan
24 Sucio
25 Camarero
27 Pollo
29 Reservar

Verticales

1 Entremeses
2 Sardina
3 Al
4 Asado
6 Bistec
10 Ajo
11 Rincón
12 Delicioso
14 Tortilla
17 Es
18 Plato
23 Jugo (*or* zumo)
25 Caro
26 Mesa
28 La
30 Va

▸▸ Extension

Pupils can go on to make their own crosswords, but this is more difficult than making wordsearches or 'trellises'. It is advisable for them to stick to short words and a small grid, and not to try to make the pattern of light and dark squares symmetrical.

35 En el mercado

page 50

It is advisable to remind pupils that they should write complete phrases in words, as in the example.

▸▸ Solution

1 *Dos kilos de patatas, por favor.*
2 *Un kilo de manzanas.*
3 *Medio kilo de tomates.*
4 *Una botella de agua mineral sin gas.*
5 *250 gramos de queso manchego.*
6 *Dos lechugas.*
7 *Una botella de vino tinto.*
8 *Una lata de sardinas.*
9 *Medio kilo de jamón serrano.*
10 *Un kilo de plátanos.*
11 *Dos barras de pan.*
12 *Cuarto de kilo de gambas.*

36 ¡Eres el intérprete!

page 51 16

The activity provides practice in understanding a business letter. All pupils can be asked to give the gist of it; the more able can translate it, using a dictionary, and then write the letter to the *Delegación Provincial de Turismo de Granada* as suggested.

▸▸ Solution

The most important points are:

The Director is sending details on campsites and youth hostels in the province. He gives the campsite names and, in brackets, the towns they are in. All are recommended. He encloses leaflets showing the classification of campsites, their facilities and charges. (He encloses a leaflet on others in the region, for interest.)

There is one youth hostel in Burgos (address and phone number given). The Youth Hostels Association can supply members with an international guide to hostels.

He also encloses a guide to hotels in the province, for interest.

The useful vocabulary on Copymaster 16 needs to be matched to the correct translation. You could provide this an an exercise.

▸▸ Solution to Copymaster 16

1 I	**6** K	**11** M
2 C	**7** N	**12** D
3 A	**8** E	**13** H
4 L	**9** O	**14** J
5 F	**10** G	**15** B

37 Perdido y encontrado

page 52 17

The vocabulary deals both with lost property and with colours. (Less frequently encountered colours are introduced: *de color rosa, naranja*.) Verbs in the imperfect are *contenía* and *había*. Both *encontrar* and *hallar* are used for 'to find'.

▸▸ Solution

A 2, **B** 6, **C** 1, **D** 8, **E** 5, **F** 7, **G** 4, **H** 3

▸▸ Extension

Pupils can also be asked to supply all the missing information and fill in the grid on Copymaster 17. This includes the colour and style of bag in each case, the precise location where each bag was lost and full details of the three items contained in each bag. See the top of page 12 for solution.

38 La colección de monedas

page 54 18

New vocabulary which should be accessible to pupils includes *penique, cero, data de* and *los años setenta*. Encourage pupils to work out *fila, siglo, suman, juntos* and *cifras*.

Pupils should attempt the clues in the order given.

▸▸ Solution

A 1949, France, 5 francs
B 1863, Britain, 1 penny
C 1942, Ireland, 1 penny
D 1963, Spain, 1 peseta
E 1971, USA, 1 dollar
F 1980, Germany, 2 marks
G 1986, Britain, 1 pound
H 1965, Italy, 100 lire

39 ¡Es un disparate!

page 56

Help pupils to suggest corrected versions of the story. Here are some possible corrections:

En la tienda de al lado (Droguería Garrigues) compré una botella de ***champú*** *y un tubo de crema bronceadora.*

Fui a la Frutería Fonseca, donde compré . . . ***dos*** *kilos de tomates.*

¿Conocéis la Farmacia Arrieta? Está ***cerca*** *de la Droguería Garrigues y la Charcutería Suárez.*

En la Panadería «Ideal» compré . . . unos panecillos ***deliciosos****.*

Entonces fui al banco . . . por diez ***libras*** *recibí dos mil* ***pesetas****. El* ***dinero me ayudó a comprar*** *mi*

▸▸ Solution to Copymaster 17

Lost by	Found by	Where	When	The bag: Colour	Style	Three items
A	2	bus stop	Tues	red	plain	pink jumper, white shoes, walkman
B	6	beach	Fri	white	writing	blue jacket, grey trousers, magazine
C	1	High Street	Sat	orange	picture	green skirt, newspaper, black shoes
D	8	bus stop	Tues	orange	picture	blue jacket, black shoes, newspaper
E	5	park	Sat	yellow	blue writing, picture	walkman, black jumper, brown shoes
F	7	High Street	Fri	red	plain	book, grey trousers, yellow blouse
G	4	park	Sat	yellow	blue writing	book, yellow blouse, black shoes
H	3	beach	Tues	white	writing	magazine, pink jumper,

billete de avión para ir de aquí a ***Londres****; el avión sale . . . el día treinta y* ***uno****.*

*Fui a unos almacenes llamados «****El Corte Inglés****» . . . para mi hermanita un paquete de* ***caramelos*** *. . . en la sección de* ***comida*** *compré* ***turrón*** *para los chicos de al lado.*

40 En el Corte Inglés

page 57

If necessary, encourage pupils to work out the meanings of *fueron, gastar, carrete, sótano, cinta, agenda*. Weaker pupils simply tick the *Verdad* or *Mentira* columns.

▸▸ Solution

The letters pupils should write down are U A N D I D E G T E R M E T A O S A P. Rearranged, they form the phrase *Guía de departamentos*.

▸▸ Extension

Ask pupils to identify examples of the preterite:

a) from the three regular conjugations (*compró, comieron, subieron*)
b) in singular and plural forms (eg, *costó, bajaron*)
c) in the negative (*no compró nada*)
d) in the reflexive form (*se compró*)

41 A la mesa

page 59

19

Pupils can enter the customers' names in any position, as long as they are in alphabetical order, anticlockwise. They can copy the list of people and items in the introduction and cross them off as they find them.

If pupils are stuck give them the following hints at appropriate points:

- Isabel has a cheese sandwich. (She doesn't eat fish or meat.)
- José likes fish, so he has fish soup and a sardine sandwich.
- Elena is opposite José (sitting anticlockwise in alphabetical order), so she has a ham sandwich.
- Isabel is the girl who has garlic soup. (Elena doesn't like it.)
- Isabel has a cold drink which is not water, so she has fruit juice. Elena must have the remaining cold drink, water.
- Isabel has garlic soup and José has fish soup. Elena doesn't like onions. So the only soup left for her is tomato.
- So Pepe must have the onion soup.
- The only sandwich left for Pepe is chicken.
- The only drink left for José is coffee.

▸▸ Solution

Elena: tomato soup, ham sandwich, mineral water
Isabel: garlic soup, cheese sandwich, fruit juice
José: fish soup, sardine sandwich, coffee
Pepe: onion soup, chicken sandwich, beer

42 Una semana en Sevilla

page 60

This is a reading and writing activity designed to practise the preterite tense. Encourage pupils to use a variety of preterite forms by asking questions such as the following:

¿A qué hora saliste de Madrid?
¿Cómo viajaste?
¿Dónde te alojaste?
¿Qué hiciste el viernes?
¿Qué comisteis?
¿Qué viste el día 17?
¿Adónde fuiste?
¿Qué lugares visitaste en Córdoba?
¿Cuánto tiempo estuviste cerca del río?
¿A qué hora volviste?
Cuando estabas con Paul, ¿condujiste tú el coche?
¿Qué hicisteis? ¿Qué tiempo hizo?
En la fiesta, ¿bailaste tú?
¿Cómo te sentiste la mañana del miércoles?
¿Te repusiste rápidamente?
¿A qué hora te levantaste para ir a Cádiz?

For extra detail, encourage pupils to find out about places of interest in Seville other than the María Luisa Park and Triana. For example:

La catedral	*La Alcazaba*
El Patio de los Naranjos	*La fábrica de tabacos*
La Torre del Oro	*El río Guadalquivir*

43 Teléfonos útiles

page 61

The activity can be done as pair work, where partners take turns to read the 'problems' and to say the corresponding phone numbers in Spanish.

▸▸ Solution

1 441 72 22 (*Tele-Ruta*)
2 441 02 14 (*Objetos Perdidos*)
3 733 22 00 or 733 30 00 (*Renfe*)
4 091 (*Policía*) or 092 (*Policía Municipal*)
5 435 22 66 (*Información del Metro*)
6 232 32 32 (*Bomberos*)
7 457 08 15 (*Grúa Municipal*), or 457 77 00 (*Guardia Civil de Tráfico*)
8 266 66 00 (*Información Ayuntamiento*)
9 411 25 45 (*Información Iberia*)
10 241 23 25 (*Oficina de Turismo*)

Note on use of glossaries: units 44 to 61

From unit 44 onwards the glossaries are accompanied by entries similar to those found in real dictionaries. The following features are used:

- Parts of speech are indicated by (*nm*), (*nf*), (*vt*), (*vi*) or (*adj*).
- Several meanings are often given, only one of which is the best in the context, eg, in unit 56, 'aseo (*nm*): cleanliness; toilet'.
- Where a word forms part of an idiom, the basic word is given first, with its meaning. It is then repeated as a dash, with the remainder of the phrase and the meaning of the idiom. For example, in unit 50:

quedar (*vi*)	to stay
~ con uno	to arrange to meet someone

- An indication of the context in which the word can be used is given in Spanish, in abbreviated form where this is dictionary usage: eg, (*Mec*), (*Ferro*), (*Ajedrez*).

You could help pupils to become used to these features by asking them:

1 to look at nouns in the glossaries for units 44 to 61 and to suggest what (*nm*), etc, stand for;

2 to look at verbs and to tell you what those with (*vt*) have in common, then to do the same with (*vi*). Give them the words 'transitive' and 'intransitive' and lead them towards a deduction of their meaning;

3 to look at some of the abbreviations for contexts and to tell you what Spanish words they stand for and what they mean, eg, *Ferro* – *ferrocarril* – railway;

4 to bring a Spanish–English, English–Spanish dictionary and find other abbreviations for parts of speech or contexts on the Spanish–English side, eg, *adv*, (*LAm*), (*Téc*). They then do the same with the English–Spanish side, eg, *n*, *adv*, *US*;

5 to look up the Spanish for a word, then to check the most appropriate meaning on the Spanish–English side, eg, 'meet': *encontrar*, *reunirse* or *conocer*?

These skills take pupils a long way towards being able to use quite complex dictionaries efficiently for themselves.

44 ¿Qué es?
page 62

The activity helps pupils to realise that they can get round the problem of unknown or forgotten words by describing the appearance or function of the item, ie, by using paraphrase.

▶▶ Extension

Give pupils the Spanish words in the solution below in random order and ask them to work out which Spanish definition each one belongs to.

▶▶ Solution

1. Electrical socket (*Toma eléctrica*) Appearance
2. Corkscrew (*Sacacorchos*) Function
3. Doorknob (*Pomo de puerta*) Appearance + function
4. Tadpole (*Renacuajo*) Appearance
5. Teapot (*Tetera*) Function
6. Picture frame (*Marco*) Function
7. Budgerigar (*Periquito australiano*) Appearance
8. Zip fastener (*Cremallera*) Appearance + function
9. Mug (*Taza alta*) Appearance
10. Ring-pull (*Anilla*) Appearance + function
11. Sponsored walk (No equivalent in Spanish) Appearance + function
12. Daddy-long-legs/cranefly (*Típula*) Appearance
13. Clothes horse/airer (*Tendedero*) Appearance + function
14. Staple (*Grapa*) Appearance + function
15. Doodle (*Garabatos*) Appearance + function
16. Mop (*Fregasuelos*) Appearance + function

45 ¿Por qué se llama así?
page 64

▶▶ Solution

Gente famosa
Plaza de la Reina Sofía
Glorieta de Goya
Paseo de Colón

Santos
Calle Santo Tomás
Avenida San Pedro
Rambla San José

Países
Avenida de Marruecos

Regiones
Parque de Galicia
Puente de Aragón

Ciudades
Carretera de Lérida
Calle de Segovia

Nacionalidades
Playa del Inglés
Explanada de los Franceses

Edificios importantes
Ronda del Alcázar
Plaza del Ayuntamiento

Fechas
Calle del Dieciocho de Julio
Plaza Dos de Mayo

Ideas abstractas
Calle Socorro
Calle de la Paz

Profesiones
Calle Carniceros

Relacionado con el agua
Calleja de la Fuente Vieja
Calle Ríos Verdes

▶▶ Extension

Ask pupils to provide English words for the types of thoroughfare within the town (eg, *carretera, avenida, calle* and *calleja*). In some cases you can ask them where they think the place is, for example *Explanada de los Franceses* is a seafront, *Carretera de Lérida* is a main road leading out of town.

They can then try to find some place names in their town which can be wholly translated (eg, *Plaza de la Ciudad* = Town Square), write them down and ask their partner to identify them.

46 Casa fundada en . . .
page 65

20

If necessary help pupils to deduce that Sra. de Nadal is at No. 2 by a process of elimination, and similarly that the baker's is at No. 1.

▶▶ Solution

1. Suárez, baker's, 1950
2. Nadal, butcher's, 1920
3. Rueda, shoeshop, 1890
4. Sotogrande, bookshop, 1980

47 ¡Es un disparate!
page 66

21

▶▶ Solution

The nonsense is:

1. • *el total será de* ***54.890*** *pesetas* (54.980 pesetas)

- *pasar unos días en el Hotel* ***Santa Bárbara*** (Hotel Estrella)
- *el veinticinco de* ***junio*** (July, not June)

2 - *se encontraba* ***debajo del restaurante*** («Mi habitación estaba en el piso más alto»)
- *necesito* ***los libros*** *que contiene*
- *me encuentro de vuelta a* ***Australia*** (Vienna is in Austria)
- *la* ***Pensión*** *Paraíso*
- ***Andalucía*** *es un lugar de ensueño para mí* (Segovia is in Castile)

3 - *tenemos muchos ganas de ver* ***la capital de nuestro país*** (The letter is written from Madrid)
- ***nuestro avión llega al aeropuerto***
- *tendremos que coger un taxi* ***hasta Barajas*** (Barajas is the airport)
- *la cuna* ***para nuestra hija***
- *siempre hemos querido visitar* ***esa catedral*** (El Escorial is not a cathedral)

4 - *para mis padres una habitación con* ***cama individual***
- *con* ***vistas al mar***
- *para* ***tres*** *personas*
- *para* ***cuatro*** *noches*
- *ambas con* ***baño***

▸▸ Extension

Pupils can gain practice in dealing with communication difficulties by writing a reply from one of the hotel keepers. First discuss the structures listed, including, if appropriate, the present subjunctive after *¿Cómo es posible que . . .*, and ask pupils to suggest others. As an example of a more elaborate reply, display Copymaster 21 on the OHP or on duplicated sheets, and discuss the structures in it.

Model answer – Letter 1

Muy señora mía:

En contestación a su carta del 30 de febrero, me ha dejado un poco perpleja.
El total será de 54.980 pesetas. El hotel se llama Hotel Estrella. Está en la ***Avenida*** *Santa Bárbara.*
Sería tan amable de aclarar este punto: ¿llega usted el 25 de junio o de julio?
Le saluda atentamente

Directora
Hotel Estrella

48 Los españoles viajan

page 68

Pupils working individually can write in English a summary of one of the sections of text. They could then translate the nine sentences, with a dictionary, and put them in the same order as they appear in the text.

▸▸ Solution

- *Si Vd. es aficionado. . . FOTOGRAFÍA Y PELÍCULAS*
- *Es mejor. . . DINERO*
- *Puede llevar. . . DINERO*
- *Deje en casa. . . EQUIPAJE*
- *En algunos países. . . PROPINAS*
- *Es aconsejable. . . DINERO*
- *Hay algunas excursiones. . . EXCURSIONES*
- *En cuanto. . . VESTIMENTA ADECUADA*

▸▸ Extension

You could ask pupils to tell you in English of other pieces of advice in the text but not in the list of nine, for example:

- Do not forget any essential document.
- Avoid carrying too much luggage.
- The weight of each suitcase should not exceed 20 kilos for air passengers, or 30 kilos for coach passengers.
- You may not take more than 320,000 pesetas out of Spain.
- Do not carry jewels or large amounts of cash.
- Wear cotton rather than synthetic clothes in hot countries.
- Wear formal clothes only in the evenings.
- Excursions are a good way to get to know the country better.
- Photographs, slides, films and videotapes make good souvenirs.

You could help the most able pupils to express some of the above in Spanish, eg, *No olvide ningún documento esencial.*

49 ¡Discúlpame!

page 69

The activity deals with apologising and explaining. Encourage pupils to examine the object pronouns in the 'excuses' to link them with the nouns in the 'complaints'.

▸▸ Solution

1 J	**5** H	**9** C
2 L	**6** B	**10** K
3 F	**7** A	**11** G
4 I	**8** D	**12** E

50 ¿Quién espera a quién?

page 71

The aim is to consolidate vocabulary associated with train travel, and the use of the regular preterite forms. There is one irregular preterite: *tuve que*. You may need to ensure pupils know the meaning of *comprobar* and are familar with the *hace . . . que* construction.

▸▸ Solution

C is meeting H
D is meeting B
F is meeting E
G is meeting A

51 El árbol genealógico

page 72

The activity deals with introductions and family relationships, and illustrates the way Spanish people add their mother's maiden name to their father's surname, use *don* and *doña*, and form pet names.

You could also point out that Spanish women, on marriage, sometimes add *de* plus their husband's name. Thus *doña Josefa* would be *doña Josefa Ruiz Fuentes de Guzmán*.

▸▸ Solution

A
1 Miguel Guzmán Arrieta
2 Juan Carlos Martínez Guzmán
3 Josefa Ruiz Fuentes
4 Gloria Guzmán Ruiz
5 Teresa Guzmán Pérez
6 Juan Carlos Martínez Guzmán
7 Carlos Guzmán Ruiz

B
1 Teresa
2 Santiago
3 Conchi
4 (doña) Josefa
5 Marta
6 Carlos y Marta
7 (doña) Josefa

52 Horóscopo

page 73

The questions increase in difficulty and can therefore be used for a wide range of ability. Before pupils attempt the activity, they could write the English equivalents of those signs which are spelled differently in Spanish (Cancer, Capricorn, Taurus, Scorpio, Aquarius, Gemini, Sagittarius, Pisces). Then ask them to write the meanings of the sub-headings (You, Friends, Love, Number, Colour, Super Day, Careful With . . .).

▸▸ Solution

The signs, with the key words or phrases, are:

1 Gemini (*Naranja*)
2 Virgo (*Jueves 21*)
3 Libra (*Sábado 30*)
4 Aquarius (*Cuidado con: Alguien con ojos azules.*)
5 Aries (*Cuidado con: Las bebidas muy frías.*)
6 Capricorn (*Cuidado con: La espalda.*)
7 Sagittarius (*Es probable que hagas una nueva amistad.*)
8 Capricorn (*Un/a amigo/a cercano/a tiene problemas monetarios.*)
9 Aquarius (*Un/a amigo/a que te prometió algo hace tiempo, cumplirá su promesa.*)
10 Leo (*Tienes que hacer un regalo y no sabes qué comprar. . .*)
11 Virgo (*No te sientes atraído por nadie en especial*)
12 Pisces (*Prepárate a conocer nuevas sensaciones.*)
13 Aries (*. . . podrías tener algunas problemas con la garganta.*)
14 Scorpio (*Te has dado cuenta de cuáles son las prioridades.*)
15 Cancer (*No te metas en más líos.*)

Examples of sentences which would provoke the exclamations are:

«¡Qué bien!» *Tu situación no es tan desesperada . . .* (Aries)
«¡Qué suerte!» *Una quincena afortunada . . .* (Pisces)
«¡Qué risa!» *Te esperan por delante unos días muy, muy apasionados.* (Pisces)
«¡Qué pena!» *. . . los amigos de verdad se pueden contar con los dedos de una mano.»* (Cancer)
«¡Qué disparate!» *Cuidado con: La luz.* (Pisces)

▸▸ Extension

Pupils could then proceed to work out the gist of the forecast for their own signs, using a dictionary. More able pupils could produce a translation of it. They could then go on to write in Spanish a short imaginary forecast which would make someone exclaim *¡Qué bien!* or *¡Qué disparate!*

You could ask pupils to find examples of the future tense (regular and irregular) and the imperative (positive and negative).

Examples of **future tense**:
Regular: se apuntará, comprobarás, aguantarás, se te presentará, sabrán, será, cumplirá, actuarás, intentará, tomarás, verás, parecerá.
Irregular: hará, tendrás.

Examples of **imperatives**:
Positive: procura, aclara, échale, presta, pide, deja, piensa, mantente, provócale, recupera, prepárate.
Negative: no te metas, no desaproveches, no te hagas, no pienses, no bajes.

53 En consigna
page 75

The activity combines work on lost property and communication difficulties. The lost item is of course 'socks' (the letters S-O-C-K-S sound like *Eso sí que es*).

Pupils can make their own words or phrases spelled in the 'Spanish' way and ask their partner to guess them. This focuses attention on the differences between Spanish and English spelling and pronunciation. Other topics which can be treated in this way are shopping, asking the way, and ordering food and drink.

▶▶ Solution and Extension

Ask more able pupils to give the equivalents of the 'English' words in Spanish, ie:

sori = sorry = *lo siento*
bótolovuain = bottle of wine = *botella de vino*
esmol = small = *pequeño*
brifques = briefcase = *maletín*
leda = leather = *cuero*
main = mine = *mío*
presens = presents = *regalos*
jevi = heavy = *pesado*
biga = bigger = *más grande*
notdátuan = not that one = *no es ése*
ódauan = other one = *el otro*
aidono = I don't know = *no sé*
los maitíquit = lost my ticket = *he perdido mi billete*
játancout = hat and coat = *sombrero y abrigo*
jóldol = holdall = *bolsa de viaje*
maiclós = my clothes = *mi ropa*
hielo =yellow = *amarillo*
oeit = wait = *espere*
perochús = pair of shoes = *par de zapatos*
jariaplis = hurry up, please = *dese prisa, por favor*
grin = green = *verde*

54 Corazonadas
page 76

First invite pupils to spot which messages are in Catalán. After giving them time to read the messages, go round the class asking individuals, eg, *¿Quién escribió un mensaje poético? ¿Quién parece ser muy contento?* Each time ask if another pupil agrees: *¿Y tú, estás de acuerdo?* You can ask for explanation in Spanish of words such as *empeñado, doliente, suplicante, enigmático.*

▶▶ Solution

The best answers are:

alegre: A.J., J.L., Jane
triste: Adriana, Pedro
dolido: Salisburio
fiel: Pochi, Richi
tímido: anonymous writer in Vilanova I la Geltrú
empeñado: Jorge
una admiradora secreta: Cristina, anonymous writer
suplicante: 'Flor de tu Tallo'

poéticos: Pochi, A. Débora, M.D.M.
concisos: Vicenç, S.
enigmáticos: Eva, Vicenç
simplemente románticos: A. Débora, M.D.M., Jane, A.A., F.M. Ch., M.T., M.D.N.

55 Crucigrama: el ocio
page 78

22

Pupils now reach the stage of tackling a full crossword, that is to say, with clues which are definitions or cryptic, and with the number of letters indicated after each clue. The crossword deals almost entirely with the topic of leisure activities and also includes verbs, articles and prepositions which enable sentences to be built.

▶▶ Solution

(See page 18.)

Possible sentences beginning *Me gusta . . .* and using each word once only, include:

Me gusta el ajedrez / el minigolf / el mar / el cine.
Me gusta ir al cine / al fútbol.
Me gusta salir con mis amigos.
Me gusta ver la tele / la película.
Me gusta nadar en el mar / la piscina.
Me gusta el baloncesto más que la vela.
Me gusta el fin de semana.

▶▶ Extension

Ask those pupils who finish before the others to make sentences other than those beginning *Me gusta . . .*, again using each word only once. You could ask the class to judge the most ingenious one, providing that it does not break the basic grammar rules.

Examples might be:
¿Opinas que el fin de semana era divertido?
Sí, el fútbol era emocionante.
Ni el ciclismo ni la vela me gusta.
¡Id al cine!
¡Reíd en el bar!
¿Lees en los cafés?
El actor cae al mar.

56 Publicidad en el metro

page 81

23

▸▸ Solution

1 soap
2 coffee
3 car hire
4 Metro
5 deodorant
6 beer
7 sherry
8 travel agent's
9 bank
10 toothpaste
11 secretarial agency
12 shampoo

57 ¡Eres el intérprete!

page 82

Encourage pupils to discuss in Spanish which of the suggestions or requests they would accept and reject. (There are no obviously nonsensical suggestions.) If rejecting, how would they do so without giving offence? Use prompts such as:

¿Confirmarías el vuelo de regreso al llegar a Bilbao?
¿Pagarías tanto dinero para aprender a esquiar?
¿Dirías a Conchita que no vas a tener bastante dinero?

58 La comida de antaño

page 84

The activity gives a different slant to the 'food and drink' topic and enables grammatical rules governing tenses, especially the preterite and imperfect, to be seen in action. It also demonstrates the simple and reflexive forms of the passive. The *encuesta* makes students aware that they possess the skill of skimming: deciding which parts of a text they will or will not read.

▸▸ Solution 55 Crucigrama: el ocio

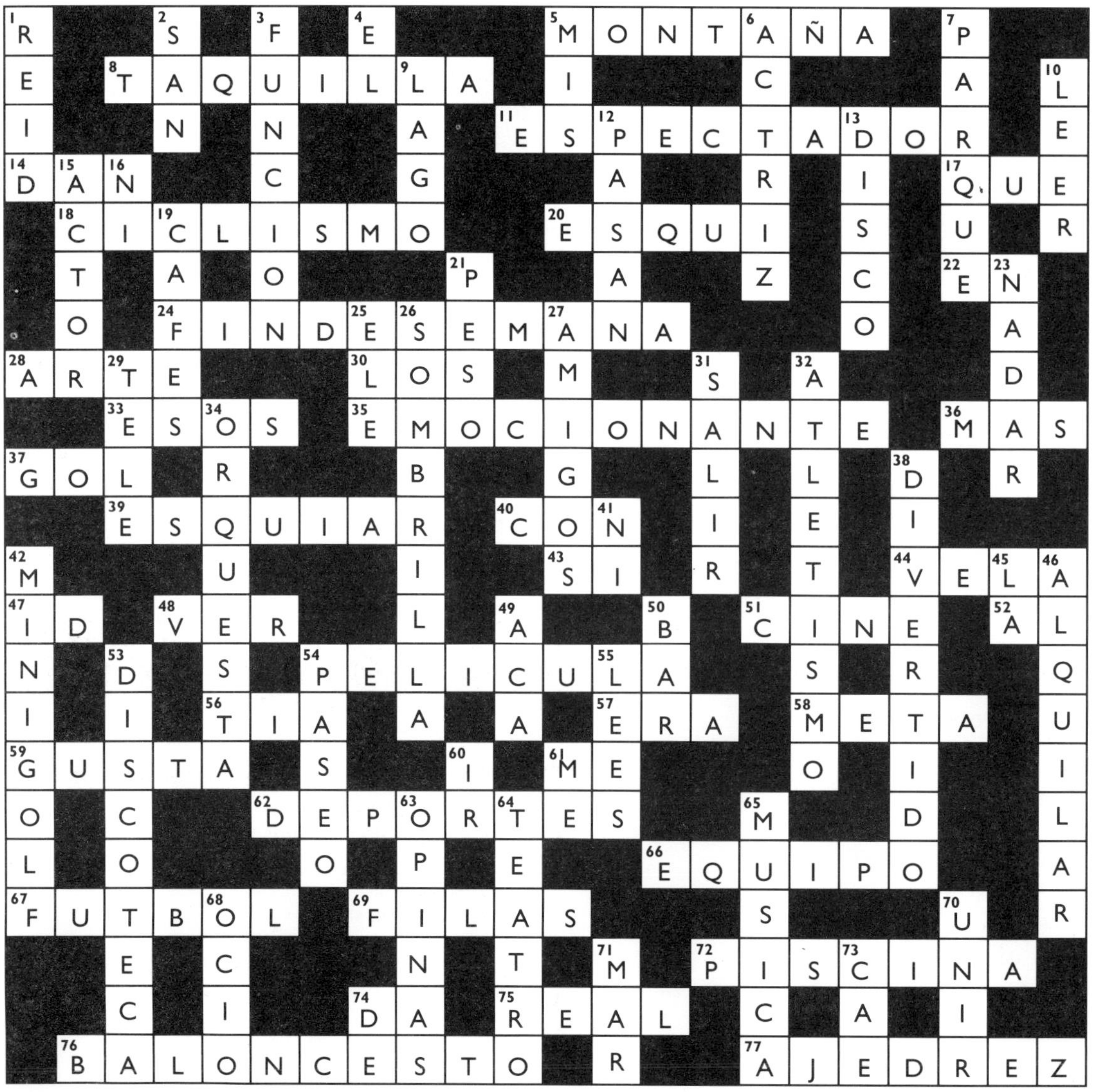

▸▸ Extension (linguistic)

Ask pupils to find in the text:

- a verb in the present
- a verb in the preterite
- a verb in the imperfect
- a verb in the pluperfect
- a verb which is in the preterite because we are told that the action took place only once
- any two verbs which are in the preterite because the action took place at a precise time or within a precise period
- any two verbs which are in the imperfect because the action was habitual
- a verb which is in the imperfect because it describes 'how things were'
- the imperfect of *hay*
- three reflexive verbs used to express the passive in different tenses
- three examples of the passive made with *ser*, in different tenses

▸▸ Solution

- There are three verbs in the present: *es* in paragraph **4**, *se cree* in **9** and *se sabe* in **10**.
- Preterites: see below.
- Imperfects: see below.
- Pluperfects: *habían sido* in **3**, *se había convertido* in **5**.
- The preterite which is accompanied by *una vez* is *bebió* in **7**.
- Some preterites with precise time scales are:

  no se comieron naranjas durante la Ultima Cena **(3)**
  eso sucedió más de 1.000 años después de la Crucifixión **(3)**
  se hizo así durante más de un siglo **(5)**
  no se popularizó . . . hasta el siglo XII **(8)**
  fueron importadas . . . a principios del siglo XVI **(9)**
  las patatas fueron prohibidos . . . en 1610 **(9)**
  esta bebida no apareció en Europa antes de 1517 **(10)**

- Some verbs in the imperfect describing habitual actions are:
  no se permitía **(1)**
  infringían **(1)**
  se acostumbraba **(4)**
  absorbía **(4)**
  se servía **(5)**
  criaban **(6)**
  se les alimentaba **(6)**
  bebían **(7)**
  volvían **(9)**
  provocaba **(9)**
  bebían **(10)**
  se importaba **(10)**
- Imperfects which best describe 'how things were' are *era* and *eran* in **2**, **6**, **7** and **8**.
- *Había* ('there was') occurs in **3**.
- Some examples of the reflexive passive in different tenses are:

  se hizo (preterite, **5**)
  no se popularizó (preterite, **8**)
  se servía (imperfect, **5**)
  se importaba (imperfect, **10**)
  se había convertido (pluperfect, **5** and **10**)
  There is also *se acostumbraba* for 'people were accustomed' in **4**.

- Some examples of the passive with *ser* in different tenses are:

  fue considerado (preterite, **1**)
  eran mantenidos (imperfect, **6**)
  habían sido introducidos (pluperfect, **3**)

59 Las profesiones

page 86

▸▸ Solution

A **7** B **3** C **1** D **4** E **9** F **8** G **2** H **6** I **5**

Like their jobs: B, C, D, E, G, H, I
Highest pay: C, E, I
Dislike their jobs: A, F
Work on Saturdays: A, B, D, F, H, I
Work at home: B, C, H, I

▸▸ Extension

Encourage pupils to discuss the careers in Spanish – *¿Te gustaría hacer eso? — ¿Por qué (no)? — ¿Estás de acuerdo con lo que dice? — ¿Qué te gustaría hacer después de terminar tus estudios?*

The nine visiting cards could be used for a sort of 'Bingo': each pupil chooses three cards and you say a sentence in Spanish about each card in random order. The first pupil to have his or her three cards referred to is the winner.

60 ¿Cuándo se dice eso?

page 90

The activity revises introductions, and accepting and declining invitations. It also teaches exclamations.

▸▸ Solution

1 (a)	**5** (d)
2 (d)	**6** (b)
3 (d)	**7** (d)
4 (a)	**8** (c)

61 Las carreras

page 91

The activity deals with training, the world of work and inhabitants of Spanish towns and cities.

Give pupils these adjectives and ask them to guess where the people come from:

albaceteño (Albacete)
alicantino (Alicante)
compostelano (Santiago de Compostela)
gaditano (Cádiz)
granadino (Granada)
madrileño (Madrid)
malagueño (Málaga)
oscense (Huesca)
ovetense (Oviedo)
pamplonica (Pamplona)
santanderino (Santander)
sevillano (Sevilla)
valenciano (Valencia)
vigués (Vigo)

Then you could ask pupils to think of words for inhabitants of cities in their own, or another, country, eg:

Bristolian
Dubliner
Glaswegian
Liverpudlian
Mancunian
New Yorker
Sydneysider

Here is an explanation of the terms used:

BUP: *Bachillerato Unificado y Polivalente* (secondary school leaving certificate, awarded at age 17)

CAP: *Certificado de Aptitud Pedagógica* (teacher-training certificate for secondary school teaching)

COU: *Curso de Orientación Universitaria* (one-year pre-university course)

The *Graduado Escolar* is awarded to those who leave school at 16 having passed all their *materias;* the *Certificado de Escolaridad* is given to those who do not pass all *materias.*

'La Mili' (*El servicio militar*) currently lasts one year and is done at age 18 if it is voluntary and at age 21 if compulsory.

►► Solution

1 Carlos Zambrano es taxista.
2 María-Ángeles Izquierdo es médica.
3 Leonor Suárez es enfermera.
4 María-José Arias es maestra.
5 Ramón Puente es albañil.
6 Octavio Salcedo es profesor.

❶ La ciudad antigua

I

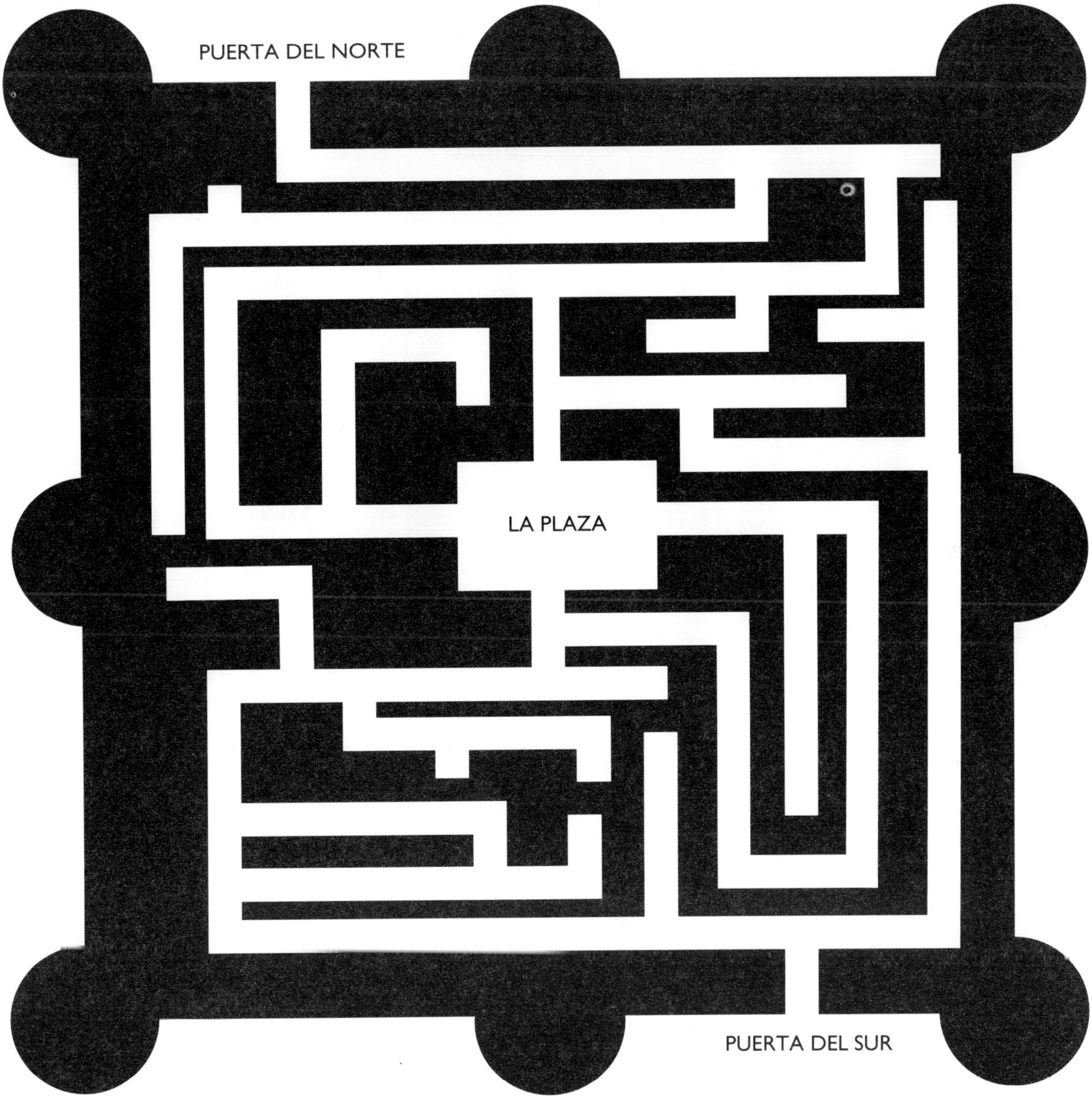

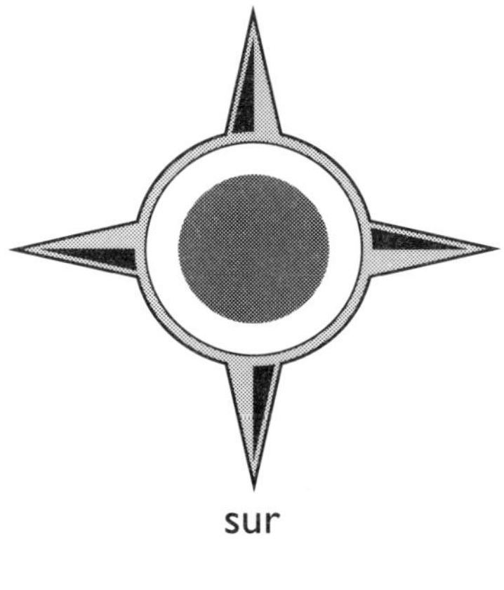

❷ ¿Abierto o cerrado?

Pueblo Pirineo

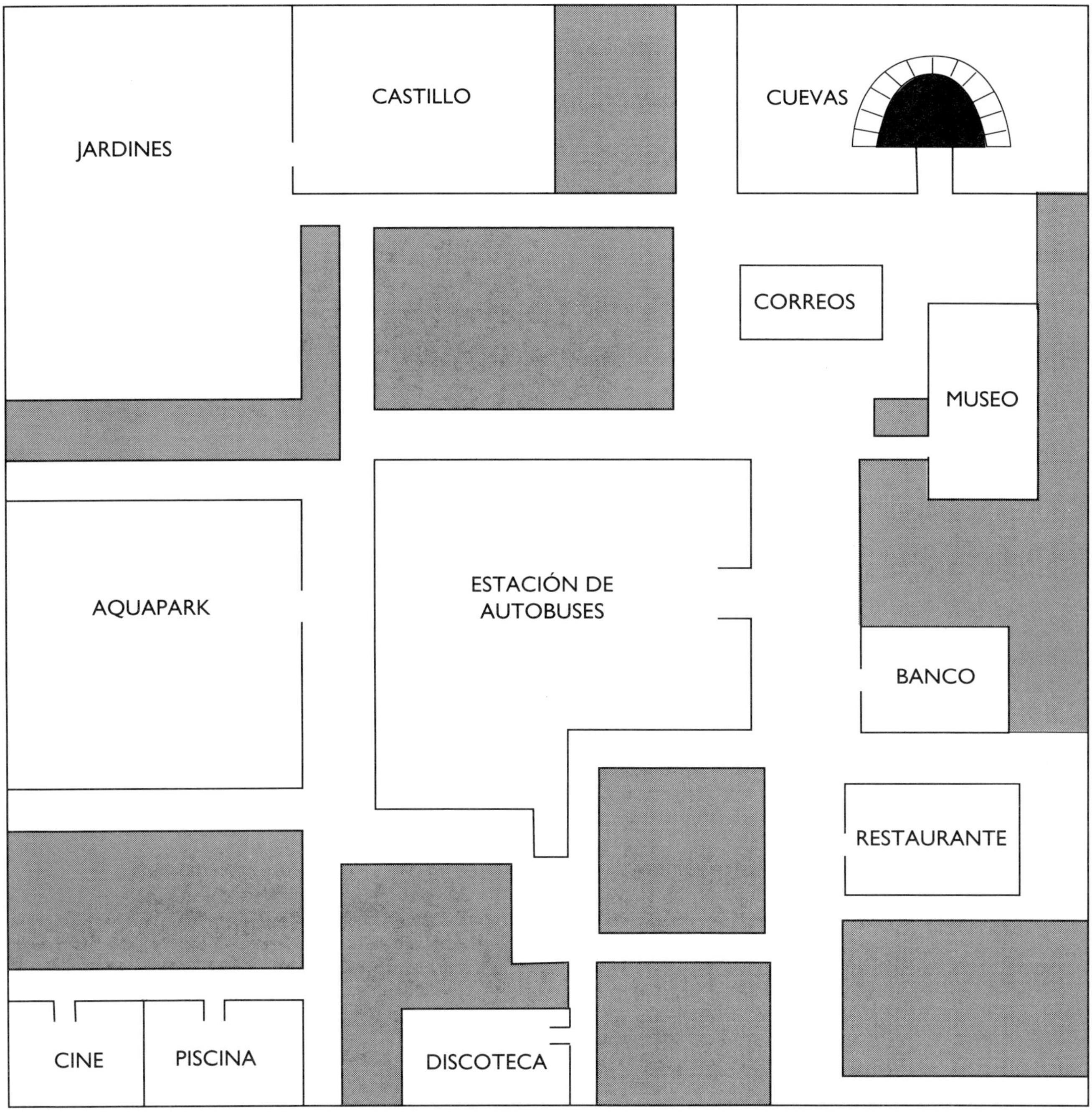

4 Unas postales

3

Complete these sentences to write postcards from Barcelona and Malgrat.

Estamos en Barcelona. Son las siete de la tarde. En Barcelona hay muchos ______________________ y ______________________. Nuestro hotel está cerca de la ______________________. En las calles hay mucho ______________________.

Estamos en Malgrat. La ______________________ es fenomenal. Es muy ______________________ y hay ______________________ cerca. El hotel está cerca del ______________________. Mañana vamos de paseo en ______________________.

⑨ La tienda de recuerdos

4

24 de Agosto

Amiga Ana:
Aquí las tiendas de recuerdos son muy buenas.
He comprado

Hasta luego,
Maribel

Srta Ana Balnes
Recoletos 84, 2° C,
La Línea,
(Cádiz)

⑩ De compras

5

	Article	Size	Colour
Antonio			
Miguel			
Luisa			
Sofía			

6

11 Correos

I	R	C	A	E	S	I	A	P
N	A	O	N	S	R	N	H	L
T	R	R	O	E	O	D	E	A
E	A	R	T	L	D	I	O	T
R	P	E	O	L	C	C	R	S
N	R	O	B	O	I	A	E	O
A	O	S	U	S	U	T	J	P
C	V	N	Z	A	D	I	N	A
I	I	E	O	C	A	V	A	T
O	N	I	N	F	D	O	R	E
N	C	C	I	O	E	D	T	J
A	I	R	G	I	S	L	X	R
L	A	D	E	N	O	M	E	A
T	S	A	T	E	S	E	P	T

7

12 Las fichas

Name ____________________

Surname(s) ____________________

Age ____________________

Nationality ____________________

Weekly pocket money ____________________

Favourite colour ____________________

Favourite number ____________________

Favourite month ____________________

Favourite day ____________________

⓭ ¿Cuántos años tienes?

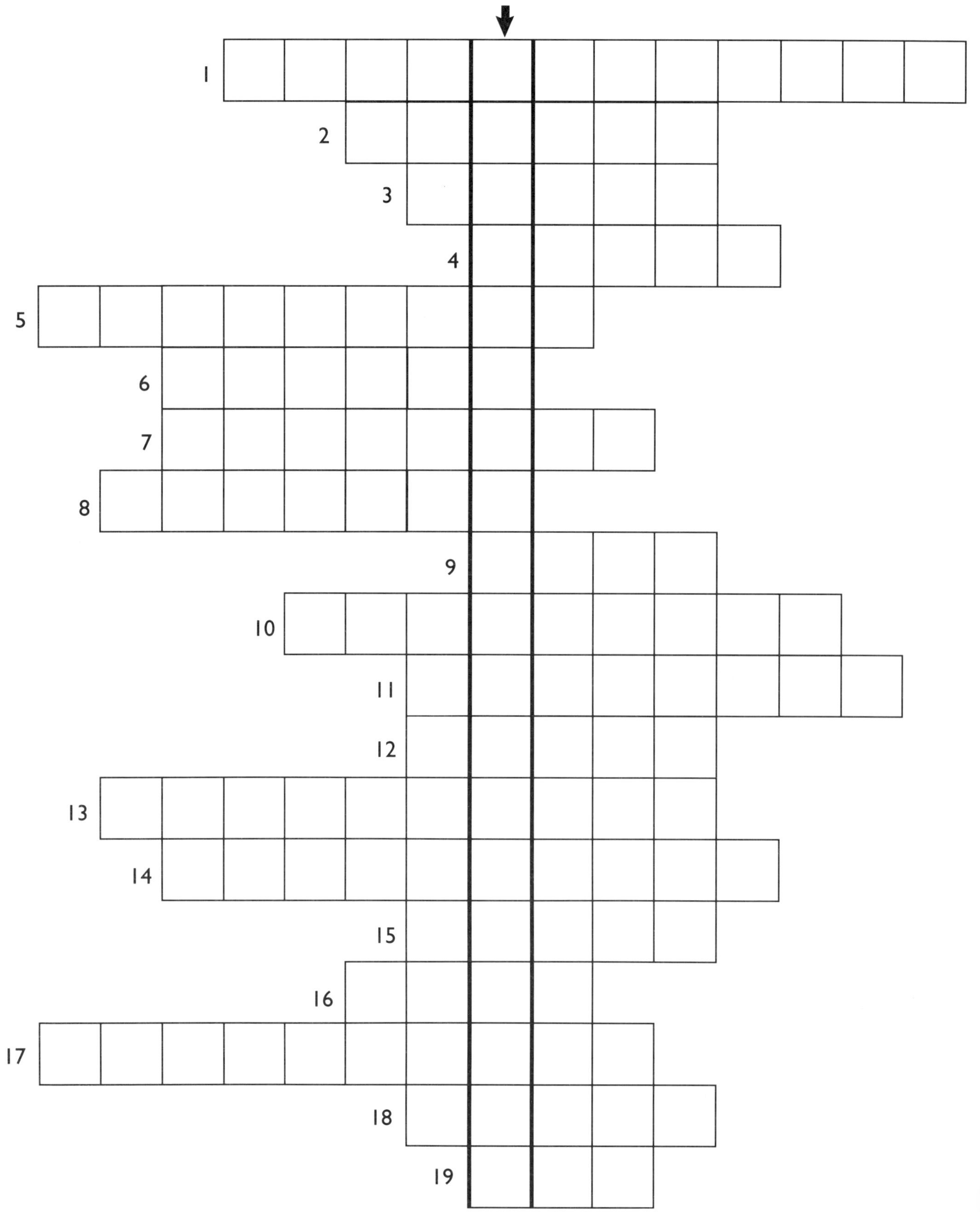

17 Busco un(a) compañero/a

Match each Spanish word or phrase with the correct English translation.

tomar parte	:	to swim
algunas veces	:	the walk
nadar	:	to take part
el lago	:	the only thing
el paseo	:	fond of tennis
la pelota	:	the lake
al aire libre	:	the team
la única cosa	:	the ball
el equipo	:	we win
aficionado al tenis	:	in the open air
ganamos	:	sometimes

21 El hotelero tiene problemas

	Room no.	**As requested?** (Tick if OK)	**Item missing?** (Tick and say what)	**Can't stay?** (If so, put a tick)
Sr. Domingo y Sr. Colón				
Sr. Olmedo, Sr. Gracián y Sr. Quevedo				
Sres. de Gredos y Pepe				
Sres. de Puente				
Sres. de Ríos				
Srta. Simón, Srta. Linares y Srta. Cobos				
Sr. Callao				
Sra. de Santos				
Sres. de Muñoz				
Rosa Muñoz				
Sres. de González y María				

23 ¿Qué le parece el hotel?

This is the hotel Comments form. Fill in the answers you think Luisa put. You can tick more than one box for question 2. Tick one box for each of the other questions, and answer questions 11 and 12 in Spanish.

Estimado huésped:

Queremos mejorar el servicio que prestamos a nuestros clientes. Por favor antes de marcharse rellene este formulario y déjelo en recepción.

La dirección

1. *¿Cómo descubrió Vd. nuestro hotel?*
- ☐ Agencia de viajes
- ☐ Publicidad
- ☐ Recomendación de otra persona

2. *¿Qué aspectos del hotel le gustan más?*
- ☐ Su situación
- ☐ Su precio
- ☐ Sus instalaciones

3. *¿Qué opina Vd. de la situación del hotel?*
- ☐ Muy bueno
- ☐ Bueno
- ☐ Regular
- ☐ Malo

4. *¿Cuál es su opinión de las instalaciones?*
- ☐ Muy buenas
- ☐ Buenas
- ☐ Regulares
- ☐ Malas

5. *¿Qué opinión tiene de la comida?*
- ☐ Muy buena
- ☐ Buena
- ☐ Regular
- ☐ Mala

6. *¿Qué piensa Vd. del servicio?*
- ☐ Muy bueno
- ☐ Bueno
- ☐ Regular
- ☐ Malo

7. *¿Qué le parece la amabilidad del personal?*
- ☐ Muy buena
- ☐ Buena
- ☐ Regular
- ☐ Deben ser más amables

8. *¿Por qué razones viaja Vd.?*
- ☐ Turismo
- ☐ Negocios
- ☐ Otra razón

9. *Viaja Vd.:*
- ☐ Con un grupo de turistas?
- ☐ Con su familia?
- ☐ Con amigos?
- ☐ Solo/a?

10. *¿Piensa que nuestro hotel representa un buen valor?*
- ☐ Sí
- ☐ Hasta cierto punto
- ☐ No

11. *¿Qué le gusta especialmente?*

____

____

____

____

12. *¿Puede indicar lo que no le gusta?*

____

____

____

Gracias por su cooperación.

26 Los vecinos

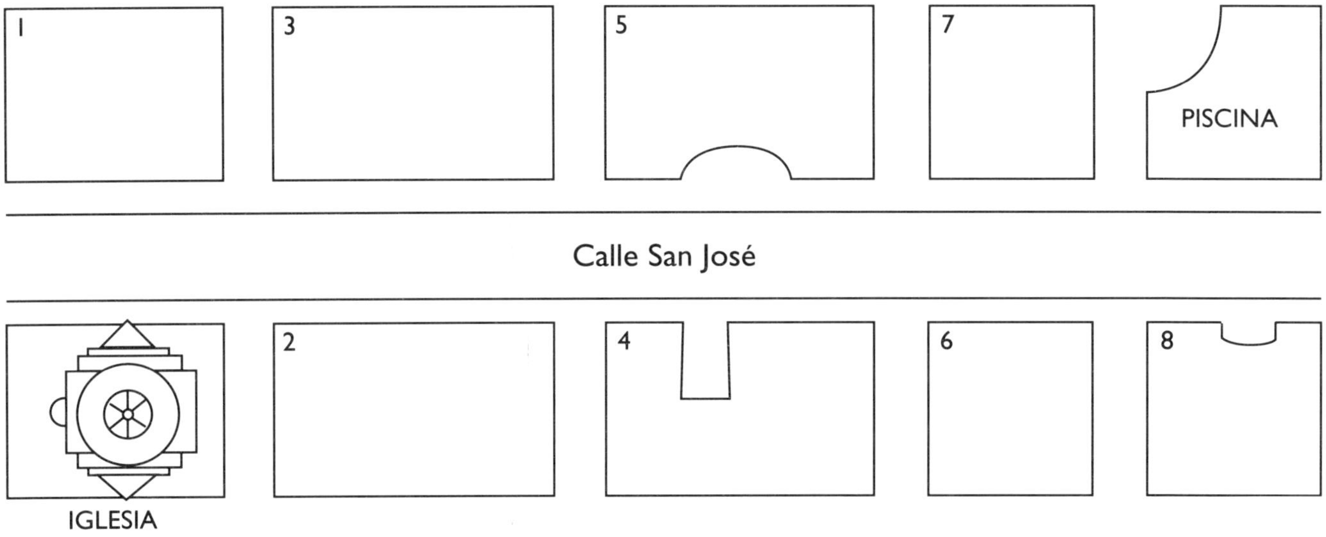

House no.	Family name	Number of children	Pets
1			
2			
3			
4			
5			
6			
7			
8			

28 Enrejado: la farmacia

14

31 Viajes

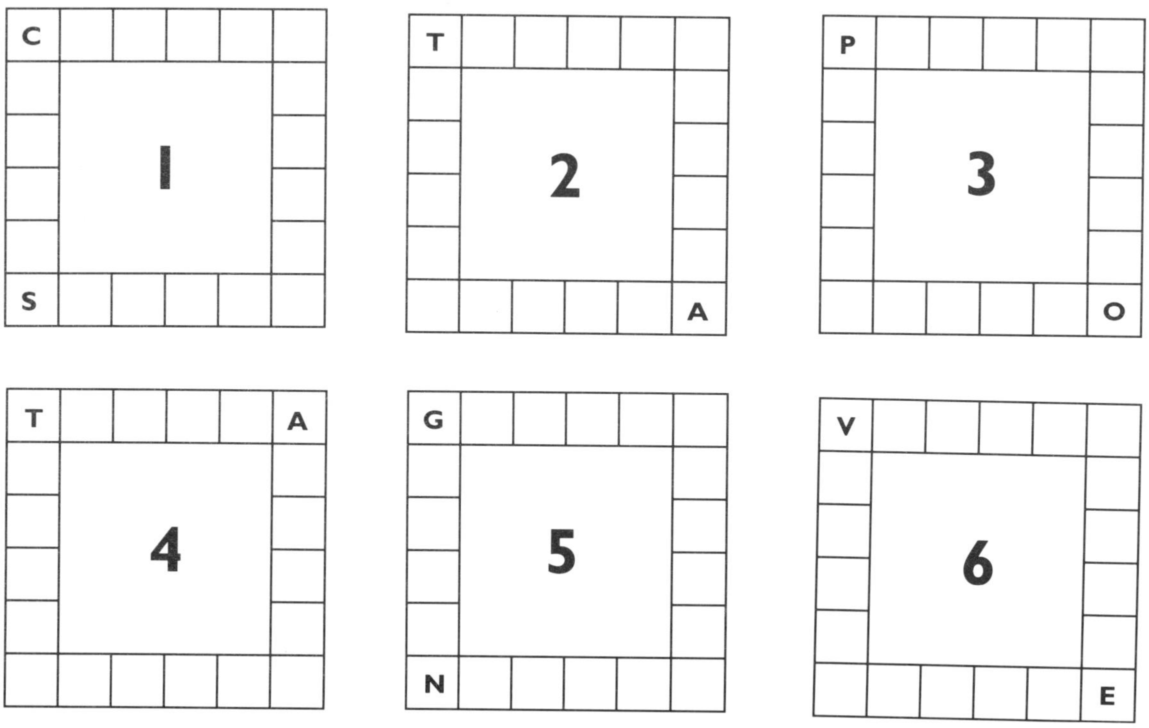

15

34 Crucigrama: la comida

36 ¡Eres el intérprete!

Match the Spanish phrase with the correct English translation.

1	**me es muy grato**	:	I enclose	A
2	**indicaciones**	:	a hotel guide	B
3	**adjunto**	:	information	C
4	**unas hojas informativas**	:	by asking for it	D
5	**para que vea**	:	neighbouring	E
6	**sus instalaciones**	:	so that you can see	F
7	**por si haya otros**	:	as for	G
8	**lindantes**	:	the headquarters	H
9	**que sean de su interés**	:	it is a pleasure for me	I
10	**en cuanto a**	:	the address is	J
11	**los socios**	:	their facilities	K
12	**solicitándolo**	:	some information sheets	L
13	**la oficina central**	:	the members	M
14	**la dirección viene**	:	in case there are others	N
15	**una guía hotelera**	:	which may interest you	O

37 Perdido y encontrado

Lost by	Found by	Where	When	The bag:		Three items
				Colour	Style	
A						
B						
C						
D						
E						
F						
G						
H						

37 La colección de monedas

18

Fill in the answers in English.

Fecha

País

Valor

A

B

C

D

Fecha

País

Valor

E

F

G

H

41 A la mesa

Fill in the answers in English.

Nombre
Bocadillo
Sopa
Bebida

Nombre
Bocadillo
Sopa
Bebida

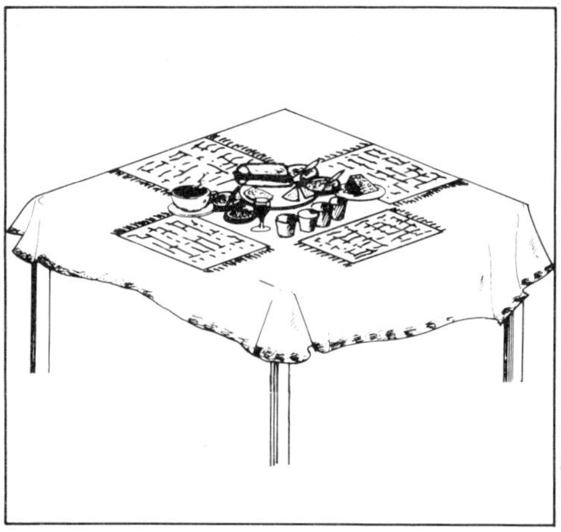

Nombre
Bocadillo
Sopa
Bebida

Nombre
Bocadillo
Sopa
Bebida

46 Casa fundada en . . .

Escribe en cada tienda, su propietario, su tipo y su fecha de fundación.

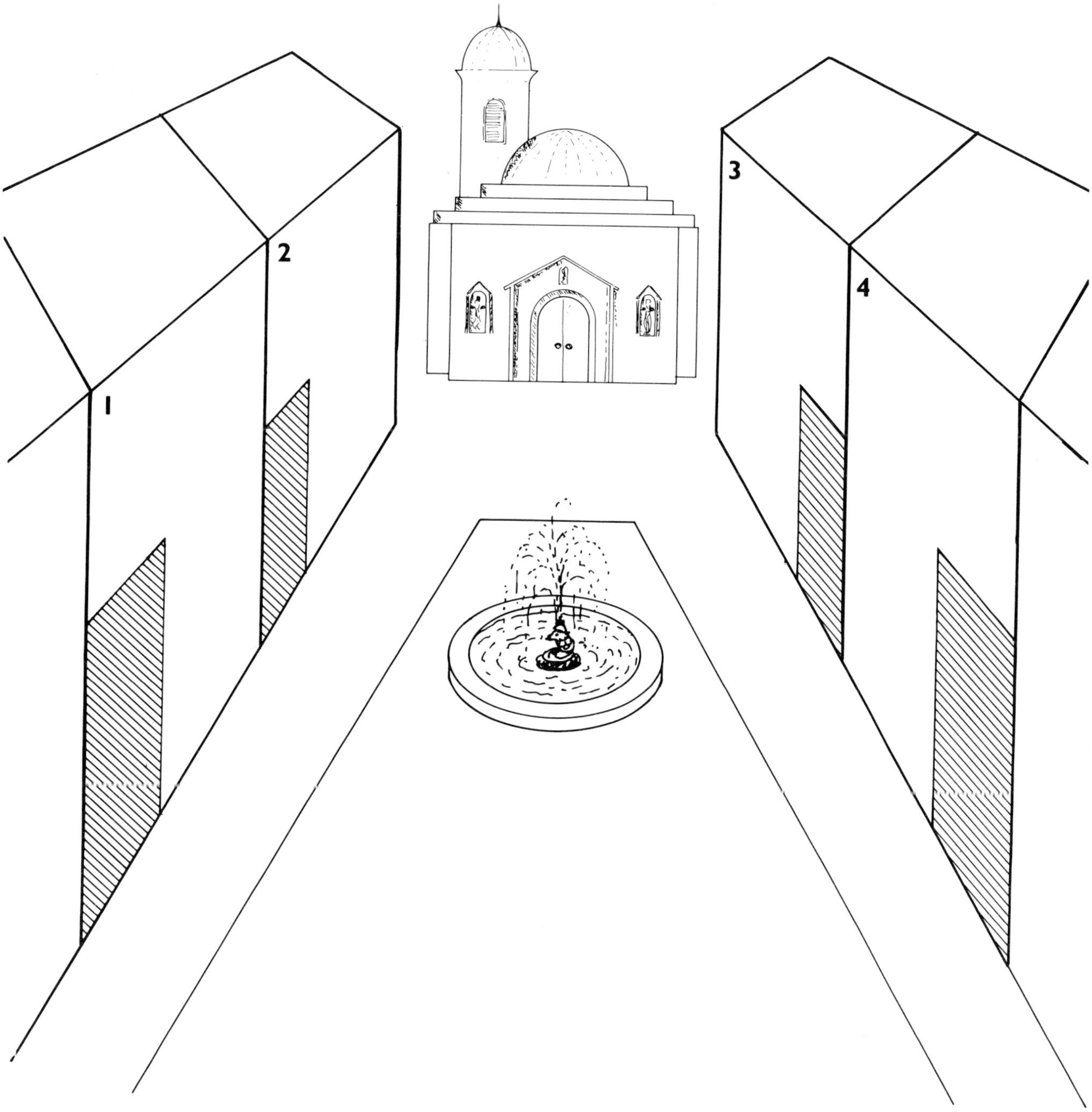

47 **¡Es un disparate!** 21

HOTEL ESTRELLA
Avenida Santa Bárbara
Alicante

Alicante, 6 de febrero

Sra. Carmen Confusa,
Calle Perdida 28, 2°,
Badajoz.

Estimada señora:

Le agradezco su amable carta de reciente fecha. (Supongo que se refería al treinta de enero, no de febrero.)

Tengo entendido que quiere reservar dos habitaciones en nuestro hotel, pero hay algunos puntos que me dejan perpleja:

1. ¿No es verdad que Vd. quiere habitaciones dobles; una para Vd. y su marido, y otra para sus dos hijos?

2. El importe total es de 54.980 pesetas, no de 54.890. Así que Vd. debe enviar un depósito de 5.498 pesetas.

3. El Hotel se llama Hotel Estrella, no Hotel Santa Bárbara. (La calle tiene ese nombre.)

4. ¿Llegan Vds. el veinticinco de junio o de julio? (Al principio de su carta dice julio, y al final junio.)

Le agradecería mucho el aclarar estos puntos; claro que no es necesario enviar las nueve pesetas que faltan.

En espera de su contestación,
La saluda atentamente

María-Jesús Hierro

María-Jesús Hierro

55 Crucigrama: el ocio

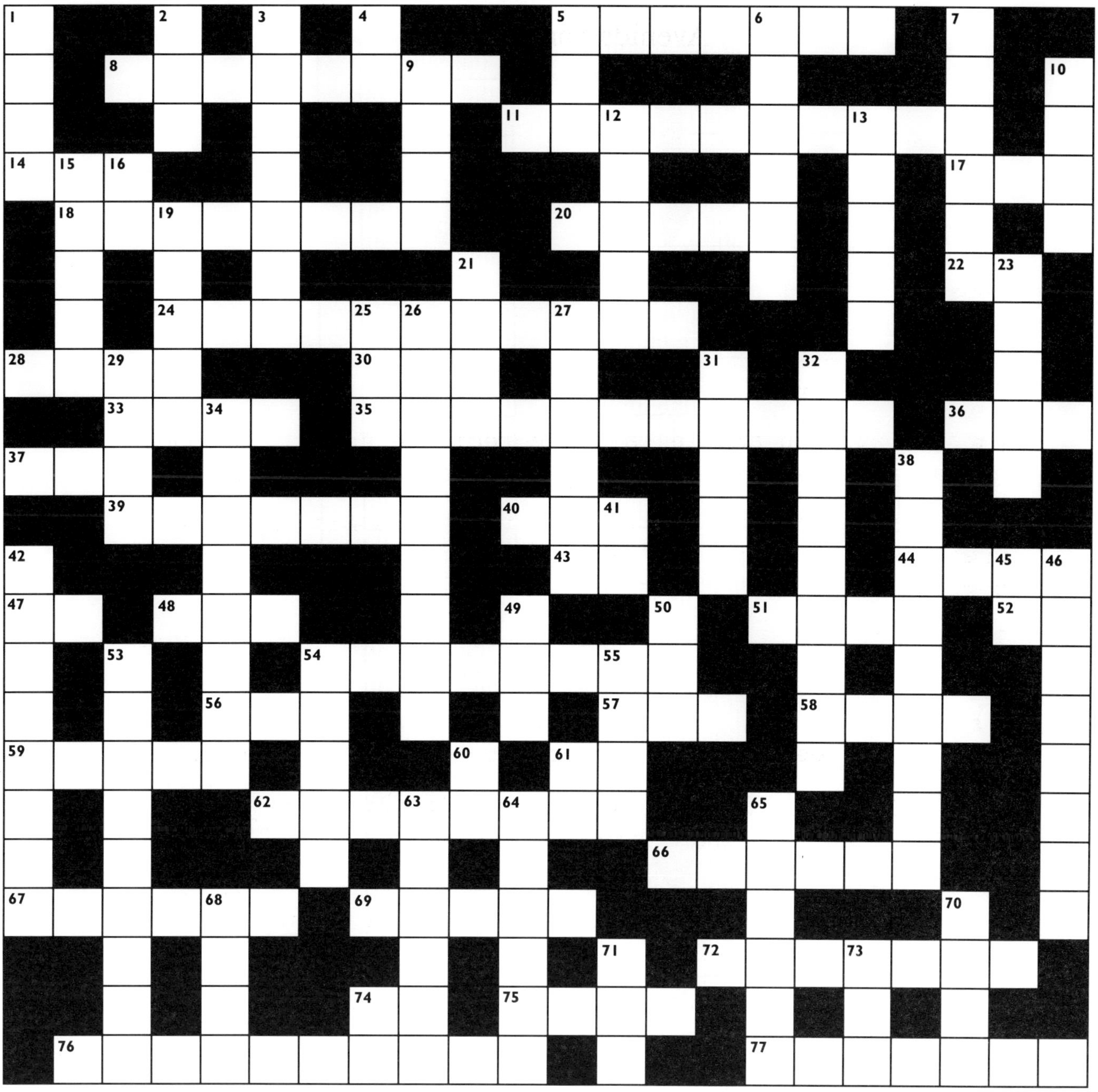

56 Publicidad en el metro

Escribe en español junto a cada número del plano lo que se anuncia allí.

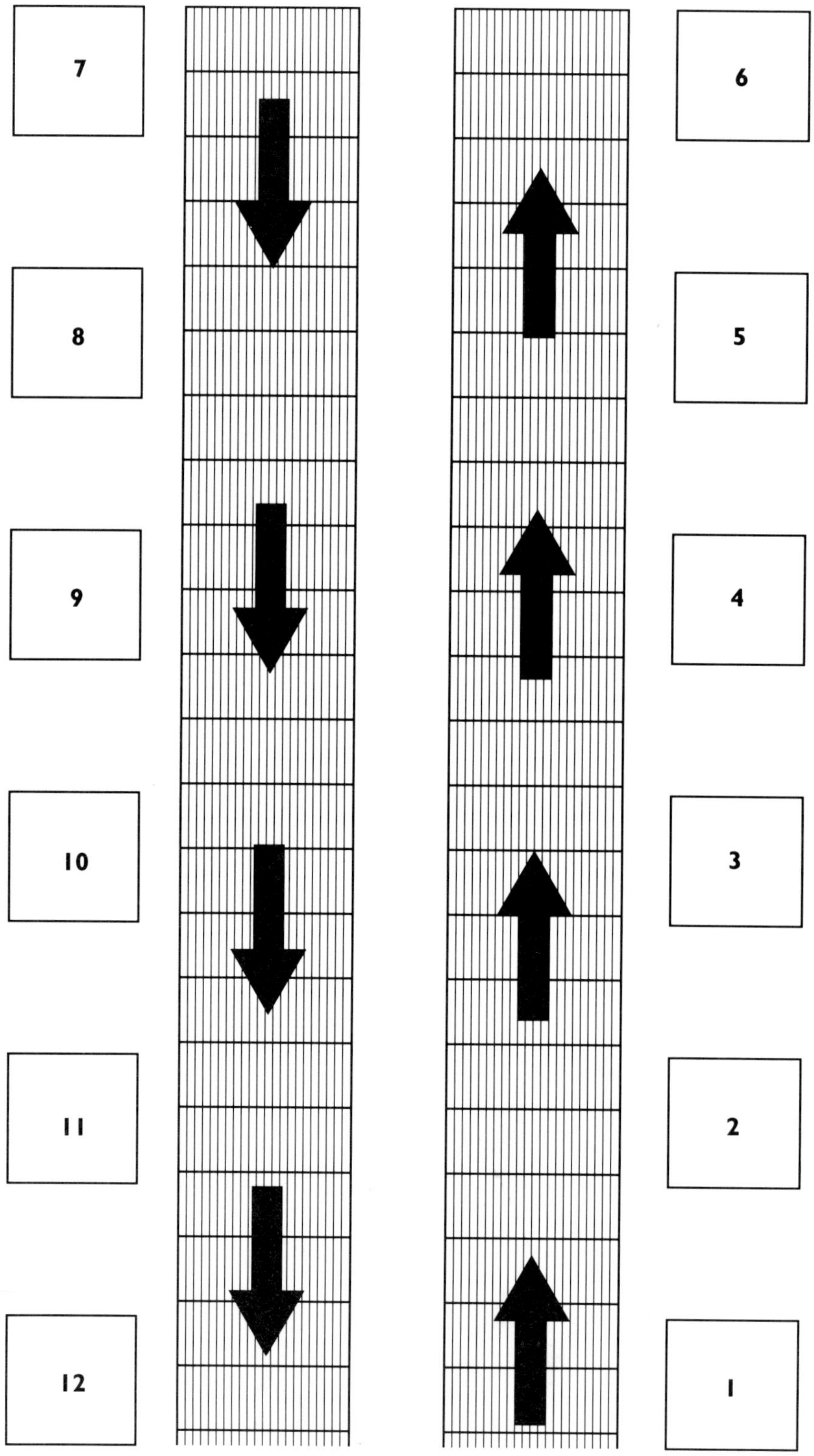